THE LIFE OF

MISS

Anne Catley

CELEBRATED

SINGING PERFORMER OF THE LAST CENTURY

INCLUDING AN

ACCOUNT OF HER INTRODUCTION TO PUBLIC LIFE

HER

PROFESSIONAL ENGAGEMENTS

IN LONDON AND DUBLIN

AND

Her Various Adventures and Intrigues

WITH WELL-KNOWN MEN OF QUALITY
AND WEALTH.

CAREFULLY COMPILED AND EDITED FROM THE BEST AND MOST
AUTHENTIC RECORDS EXTANT.

LONDON.

1888.

The Life of
Miss Anne Catley.

First published, London, 1888.

Republished Travis & Emery 2010.

Published by
Travis & Emery Music Bookshop
17 Cecil Court, London, WC2N 4EZ, United Kingdom.
(+44) 20 7240 2129
neworders@travis-and-emery.com

Hardback: ISBN10: 1-904331-91-2   ISBN13: 978-1-904331-91-9
Paperback: ISBN10: 1-904331-92-0   ISBN13: 978-1-904331-92-6

Anne Catley, Soprano. 1745-1789.

She was taught by William Bates and Charles Macklin. Her career
was focussed Dublin and London. She had some three children
before she lived with and possibly married Francis Lascelles by
whom she had a further eight children. Judging from this book and
other sources, she had quite a reputation.

More details available from
- Stanley Sadie: The New Grove Dictionary of Music and Musicians.

MISS ANN CATLEY.

Taken at the Age of Thirty.

THE LIFE OF

MISS

Anne Catley

CELEBRATED

SINGING PERFORMER OF THE LAST CENTURY

INCLUDING AN

ACCOUNT OF HER INTRODUCTION TO PUBLIC LIFE

HER

PROFESSIONAL ENGAGEMENTS

IN LONDON AND DUBLIN

AND

Her Various Adventures and Intrigues

WITH WELL-KNOWN MEN OF QUALITY
AND WEALTH.

CAREFULLY COMPILED AND EDITED FROM THE BEST AND MOST
AUTHENTIC RECORDS EXTANT.

LONDON.
1888.

Memoir of Miss Anne Catley.

NNE CATLEY, the subject of the following Memoir, was one of the most celebrated actresses of the latter half of the last century. Her personal beauty, her high vocal abilities, and her connection with certain well-known personages of the upper class, acquired for her a notoriety that was certainly distinguished, if not altogether enviable.

Various writers having expressed themselves very differently as to this lady's character, it will be interesting to gather together and present in a consecutive narrative such authentic facts as are procurable.

An author living at the time she flourished speaks of her as "at present justly the most celebrated for her musical powers the British Theatre ever boasted," and says, "she is the daughter of a hackney coachman who lived near Tower Hill." All accounts of her seem agreed about this, and that she was born in the year 1745, as the writer says, "like a bright orient gem, when removed from the dark bowels of the earth, emerging from an obscure and gloomy alley in the neighbourhood of Tower Hill. Her father," he says, "if he could not boast of luxury himself, most essen-

tially contributed to the enjoyment of it in others. His
courses were generally *above* the vulgar level, for he was
in short, and in plain English, neither more nor less than a
gentleman's *coachman*." As to the particular occupation
of the mother, opinion is much divided, but the most preva-
lent is that she was an humble *washerwoman*, and earned
small sums in that way by keeping clean the officers upon
the Tower duty.

In her infancy the little Nancy displayed charms which
attracted the attention of every beholder. Her complexion
was as fair as alabaster, her eyes sparkling; she had
vermilion lips, and nothing could equal the bloom which
adorned her cheeks. In a word, Nature seemed in forming
her to have meant to shew the world an abridgment of all
human perfection. Not to dwell, however, too long on a
subject which can afford our readers but little pleasure
besides a first perusal, we shall proceed to relate the
remarkable events of her younger years, observing only
that her beauty increased with her age.

Her education was such as persons who move in the
same sphere of life with her parents usually bestow on
their children. She imbibed the first rudiments of reading
in a charity school. She passed her youth in childish
amusements peculiar to that age, and in the company of
her equals; whom, whether male or female she strove to
excel in the noble arts of spinning a top, playing at
marbles, running down Tower Hill, jumping over posts, &c.

She had reached her fourteenth year, when, as she was
sitting one day in an alehouse, among her companions,
she was desired to sing a song. A draught of beer soon
gained her compliance, and a gentleman well known in the
musical world happening to pass by the door at that

instant, was so much attracted by the angelic though untutored melody of the little Catley that he stopped to hear her song out. When she had done he went into the house, sat down, and with the bribe of a few halfpence prevailed on her to repeat it, and when she had finished he went away without saying anything to her at that time.

He immediately enquired in the neighbourhood where her parents lived, and what business they followed; of which particulars being informed, he went to them, told them how much he admired their daughter's musical talents, and offered to take her under his tuition, and perfect her in an art for which nature had so well qualified her.

Her father and mother, overjoyed at a proposal which seemed so advantageous to their child, readily consented. Accordingly, she removed next day to the house of her patron, Mr. Bates, who put her to school very remote from the haunts of her former companions.

Here she remained some time, wholly employed in learning to read and write. After she was taken from school she applied herself with so much assiduity to acquire a competent knowledge of music, that at the end of two years she was capable of occupying a distinguished position in a London orchestra.

While living in the neighbourhood of the Tower, she became an object very much admired, and by the credulity of her unsuspecting parents was permitted to expose her budding beauties, and, as we have seen, her melodious cadences, in the commonest places of resort in that district. She was yet too young for serious love affairs, but the military heroes of the locality had their eyes upon her, as beasts of prey watch their destined victims until they arrive at a proper time and place to spring upon them. They were all, however, disappointed; Nan, before she arrived at her second teen, listened to the love-lore of a young linen draper in the Minories, and in a very short time returned his passion with equal ardour.

And now that charming voice for which she afterwards became so justly celebrated began to increase in strength and melody; insomuch that, at the recommendation of some friends, Mr. Bates gladly accepted her as an apprentice by indenture, with a penalty of £200 for the father in case of misconduct.

Upon attaining proficiency she made her first appearance in public at Vauxhall in the summer of 1762; and on the 8th of October in the same year she appeared for the first time on the stage at Covent Garden, in the character of the Pastoral Nymph in *Comus*, and gained uncommon applause.

Bates and Catley, however, soon found they could not agree. She had discovered a mortal dislike to her master, and her conduct became most irregular. It was in vain he solicited and threatened—at one time he declared that he would turn her out of doors and sue her father for the £200—in vain also were her father's entreaties, her conduct became so irritating that at last Bates agreed to allow her £25 a year for her board and lodging, and take her salary to himself. This arrangement, however, did not long continue.

The succeeding year she became an object of public attention from a very remarkable circumstance. Sir Francis Blake Delaval, one of the most notorious and abandoned characters of the times, being charmed with her beauty, and understanding that the master and his fair apprentice could not agree, resolved on releasing her entirely from the coercion of Bates, and making her his mistress. Accordingly, it was agreed that Sir Francis should pay Bates the penalty of the father's bond, and also give him £200 more in lieu of what she might earn for him by the engagement that he had made for her with the managers of Covent Garden Theatre and Marylebone Gardens. In this purpose Mr. Fraine, an attorney, was ordered to draw up a proper transfer of her indentures from Bates to Sir Francis, and she and her mother were removed into lodgings, where she lived publicly with Sir Francis, was attended by his servants, and rode out with him every day.

The attorney, having made the father a party to the articles, waited on him to have his signature and seal. Mr. Catley lived at this time with the very respectable Mr. Barclay, of Cheapside, and, having got possession of the articles, consulted his master on the nature of them.

The honest Quaker, shocked at the wickedness of transferring a girl by legal process, for the purpose of prostitution, advised with his Lawyer, who laid a case before Counsel, and the ensuing term two motions were made in the Court of King's Bench on these articles : the first of these motions was for *Habeas Corpus*, directed to Sir Francis Blake Delaval, to bring the body of Anne Catley into Court ; and the second was for a rule to shew cause why an information should not be filed against Sir Francis Blake Delaval, Bates the Master, and Fraine the Attorney, for a conspiracy to prostitute Anne Catley, under the forms of Law. On the following day, Catley, in consequence of the *Habeas Corpus*, appeared in Court, accompanied by Sir Francis, and was discharged out of his custody. The affidavits for the prosecutor were read, and a day was fixed for cause to be shewn.

On the young lady's release, her father attempted to seize her, and carry her off by force. Sir Fletcher Norton, Counsel for Sir Francis, immediately complained to the Court, and the violent conduct of the father was severely reprimanded by the Chief Justice, Earl Mansfield, who observed, that though the girl was not of legal age, she was at full discretion ; and the question being put, whether she would return with her father, or Sir Francis, she declared her attachment to the latter, put her hand under his arm, and making a curtsey to the Judges, and another to the Bar, walked with him out of Westminster Hall to his carriage, which waited at the gate, and carried them home.

On cause being shewn, the Court were clearly of opinion that the information should be granted. Lord Mansfield observed, that the Court of King's Bench was *custos morum* of the country ; and had authority, especially where the offence was mixed with conspiracy, to punish every thing *contra bonas mores.* He called the money given by Sir Francis to Bates, *premium prostitutionis*, and cited the case of Sir Richard Sedley, in the reign of Charles II. to support it.

The consequence of this information against Sir Francis, Bates, and Fraine, was a trial, and all the defendants being found guilty by the Jury, were severely fined ; the whole expense of which, together with the costs to a very considerable amount, fell upon Sir Francis.

The story of her conquest of Sir F. B. D. is told as follows, in a pamphlet published during her life-time and professing to contain many curious anecdotes never before published. She is thus described on the title page—

> " Queen of Song, of Dance, of Sports,
> You scarce will meet her like again."

Singing at Marylebone Gardens, her beauty, joined to her superior excellence in singing, could not fail of creating her a great number of admirers. Among the rest of her numerous votaries, Sir F. B. D. obtained the preference. He took her home with him in his chariot one night from the gardens.

She was not ignorant of the conquest her charms had made, and was resolved to make the utmost advantage of it. The Knight who loved her to desperation, on their arrival at his house, asked her on what terms she would consent to live with him. She heartily replied, that the happiness of being loved by him was, in her opinion, a sufficient reward for any favours that she could bestow. Pleased with this answer, he presented her with a diamond ring which he took from his finger, worth a hundred guineas, as an earnest of what he intended to do in the future.

Her conversation during supper was witty, spirited and enlivening ; she sung him several songs, all of which were on the subject of love and omitting nothing that she thought likely to increase his passion for her, the evening was passed in the most agreeable manner imaginable.

The next day he sent for his coachmaker, and ordered him to make for her a very elegant equipage. He fixed her in genteel lodgings at two guineas per week, and assigned her an allowance of five guineas.

Our heroine seemed now arrived at the pinnacle of her glory, her inamorata was too fond to deny her anything she asked him. She also, on her part resolved to give him every satisfaction in her power, and accordingly requested the favour of him to accompany her to a house near Hampstead, prepared by her appointment, to partake of an entertainment she had provided. She forgot nothing that might make everything agreeable to him; the most delicate viands and the choicest wines were served up with a degree of elegance, which plainly shewed that the mistress of the feast was no novice in the art of doing the honours of the table with propriety. All the time they sat at table, two bands of music composed of the most celebrated vocal and instrumental performers, played and sung. The knight was in raptures, but his fair flame desired him to forbear being so lavish in his thanks till after supper, when she hoped to present him with a scene that would be more deserving of them.

Miss Catley made a short meal, and retired somewhat abruptly. This behaviour surprised her lover, and he waited the issue of the event with impatience. When the things were removed she sent a servant to desire Sir F. to walk into a large hall below stairs, where a theatre appeared, representing a forest at a distance, with a beautiful valley stretching out towards it. Fields and orchards seemed in full bloom; the rivulets wandered along, and their banks were decked with woodbines and roses.

Here our heroine, who had only retired to dress, appeared as Celia asleep; three shepherds came slowly forward, the music playing, and one of them sung as follows—

> Soft advances let us make
> Towards my lovely enemy ;
> Let us, let us not awake
> Her sleeping cruelty.

Then all three sang the following trio—

> Sleep on, and take that sweet repose,
> Ye bright victorious eyes,

Which the hard law that you impose
  To other hearts denies.

STREPHON.

Silence, ye birds, ye zephyrs, peace,
  Let all a sacred silence keep;
Ye purling streams, your murmurs cease,
  For 'tis Celia that's asleep.

TRIO.

Sleep on, and take the sweet repose,
  Ye bright victorious eyes,
Which the hard law that you impose
  To other hearts denies.

This was sung admirably well; and when the shepherds had done, several shepherdesses came out of the wood. They advanced to the sleeping beauty in graceful measure, as the music played, and when they came to the bank of flowers she reclined on, one of them sang, incomparably fine, these words—

Come, Celia with your charms,
  Come view the innocent delights,
To which, with smiles and open arms,
  Our peaceful wilderness invites.
Here seek no grandeur of a Court,
Love's alone our harmless sport:
Love crowns the night, love crowns the day,
And love's the burthen of the lay.

Here Celia awakened, and, singing, said to Strephon, who stood gazing on and admiring the wonders of her face,

O what cruelty you shew,
To follow me where'er I go!

STREPHON.

Whom would you have me, fair, pursue,
But she, alas! I love—but you ?

CELIA.

What is it, shepherd, that you mean ?

STREPHON.

Fair shepherdess, I mean to die ;
    Die at your feet and end my pain,
Since at your feet I sigh.

CELIA.

Hence, Strephon, hence, I fear that I shall prove
Pity within my breast transform'd to love.

STREPHON.

    Or from pity or from love
      It is graceful to be tender !
    Shepherdess, enough you've strove,
      To his flame you must surrender.
    Or from pity or from love,
      It is graceful to be tender.

CELIA.

    Too long I've been, too long, severe,
      Your ardent vows have treated ill ;
    Here, take my heart, here, Strephon, here,
      Of just revenge here take your fill.

STREPHON.

O heavens ! O shepherds ! O Celia, why
Transport me thus ? If joy can kill, I die.

DAMON.

This prize is worthy of thy fidelity ;
Thus blest, who but must envy thee !

This scene of a comedy ballet was finely performed and
beautifully improved by the conclusion taken from Shake-
speare's *Tempest ;* that is, when the shepherds had done,
Juno, Iris and Ceres appeared, descending in a machine
of clouds, to bless this pair, and sung their blessings on
them. Iris called the Naiads of the winding brooks, by

command of Juno, summoned the sun-burnt sicklemen to put their rye-straw hats on and encounter those other nymphs in country footing. The nymphs and reapers appeared in a moment properly habited, and concluded the scene with a graceful dance.

In this manner the time passed away till midnight, the next day was passed in much the same manner, and he stayed with her about a week, and she every day entertained him with some new species of diversion. At the end of that time he took his leave, and gave her fresh tokens of his affection.

A writer in the " History of the English Theatre " (1789) says, " To the man of her choice she was faithful, loving and submissive." This opinion is certainly not borne out by facts, and another writer of her times says, " Though of a sprightly disposition and apparently of a volatile spirit, she never lost sight of her own interest." Sir Francis had possession of her person, but was never master of her heart, and there is no doubt, but that even while she resided with him, and appeared in public as his mistress, she privately engaged in intrigues with others for pecuniary consideration. A diamond to her was as inestimable an argument as to Madame Sc-l-e-g. It won her last favour as effectually as it gains the old German's interest. Her passions were strong, but she was totally destitute of sentiment and delicacy, and always gratified her appetite with a view to her interests as well as to her taste ; being attached to the whole sex without harbouring a particular fondness for any particular individual, she measured love by profit, and enjoyed indulgence without the least relish for mental satisfaction.

Macklin was the person who first discovered her talents

for the stage, and she cultivated them under his tuition with assiduity and success; for notwithstanding she pleased most when least natural and most *outre*, yet there was great capability in her mind; she could assume chaste acting, and executed many characters of difficulty with critical justice.

Time, possession, and infidelity—the capricious girl having confessed to an improper intimacy with no less a personage than the Duke of York himself, whom she declared to be the father of her third child, adding with her native pleasantry, a hope that he might be wiser than his father——having at last cooled the passion of Sir Francis, he effected an emancipation from the fascinating chains of his mistress, who, by the advice of her venerable instructor, the father of the stage, made a trip to Ireland.

It is evident that while she was making her most fervent protestations of affection for Sir F., she could not confine her desires to him alone, but among other adventures listened to the overtures made her by a rich Portuguese Jew merchant. Her amour with him seemed to be founded more on interest, than any other motive, and was as follows.

She had been kept by Sir F. about a twelve month, when returning home in a hackney chair from a visit pretty late in the evening, a foot-pad presented a pistol to the foremost man, commanding him in the usual phrase to stand. A voice at that instant cried out, "hold villain, on your life I charge you hold! dare to repeat your insolence, and this moment shall be your last." The robber obeyed, and a gentleman, richly dressed, having ordered the chairman to carry the lady home, escorted her thither himself.

As soon as she arrived at the door of her own house he handed her out of the chair, and being struck with her beauty he asked permission to pay her a visit, which she readily complied with.

He then respectfully took his leave and went home, ruminating all the way on the pleasure he was likely to reap from this happy encounter.

Before we proceed any further in the relation of this adventure, it will not be amiss to give the best account we could learn of this new adorer of our heroine. He was a native of Lisbon, his name, Miguel Diaz Fernandes ; he was very rich, and a widower. He had no children, and was about fifty years old. As to his person, he was tall and meagre, of a sallow complexion, and had something rather forbidding in his countenance. Having given this description of him, we shall resume the thread of the story.

As soon as he went home he retired to bed, but could not sleep. He lay awake the whole night, ruminating on what had passed; he arose early in the morning, and despatched his servant with the following *billet* to Miss Catley.

" Divine creature !

I am dying for love of you, and unless you take pity on me, and condescend to receive this declaration of my passion favourably, I must inevitably fall a victim to the ardent flame with which I am fired. I have sixty thousand pounds, besides a large estate in Portugal, which I here offer to make you sole mistress of. Deign therefore to give me permission to hope I am not disagreeable to you. My servant will deliver your answer to me.

I am, charming miss,

Your sincere admirer,

M. D. FERNANDES."

To this passionate epistle our heroine, when she had perused it, thought proper to send the following answer—

"Sir,

Your behaviour last night convinces me that you are a man of honour and a gentleman. As such I shall always esteem you. I know not how to look on you in any other light at present. An interview perhaps may determine me more in your favour. But oh! I fear to trust my too credulous heart. You have therefore leave to visit me at my own house this afternoon, at six o'clock. Pray come alone.   Yours,

ANNE CATLEY."

The merchant's heart was filled with joy at the receipt of this favourable answer, and he waited with the utmost impatience for the happy hour which was to make him the most blest of all mankind. Time seemed to move with leaden wings, but at length the wished-for moment came, when he mounted his chariot, which soon conveyed him to the abode of his charmer.

Being arrived at her house, she received him with an air of affected modesty, which, though it did not utterly discourage him, yet easily made him perceive that his success would cost him some pains. He was somewhat puzzled at the singularity of her behaviour, which was easy without betraying too much freedom. He was as anxious to turn the conversation on the topic of love as she seemed studious to avoid it. At length, after having, as she thought, thoroughly sifted her inamorata's inclination, she appeared all at once to comply with his wishes, and in order to give him the most exalted opinion of her virtue, invented the following tale—

"I am, sir," said she, "the daughter of an Irish gentle-man, a merchant, a native of Dublin, who, dying whilst I was very young, left me to the care of my mother, who was at that time about five-and-twenty years old. I was his only daughter, and he was so excessively fond of me that I was indulged in every reasonable wish my little heart could form; I was sensibly afflicted at his death, and used to mingle my tears with those of my mother, who bewailed his loss in the most affectionate manner imaginable. This fond parent did not survive my father above three months, and left me an orphan, with £10,000 to my portion, to the guardianship of a rich old uncle, who, when I had attained the proper age, endeavoured by threats and promises to force me to give my hand to his son, a dissolute youth, who had already deceived several young women by promising them marriage, only with a view to ruin them more easily. Finding me averse to his will, he forcibly kept from me the writings of my estate, and I, for want of friends, being unable to recover them, he gave them to his son, who in about two years squandered away all my fortune in extrav-agancies, and left me, a wretched being, reduced to the cruel necessity of earning my bread by the labour of my hands.

Having received an education suitable to the large fortune I was born to possess, I was unacquainted with, as well as incapable of undertaking, any laborious employ-ment. The place, therefore, of governess to a young lady of quality, which fortunately happened at that time to be vacant, seemed the best adapted to my abilities. I applied four years in the family, where I gave such satisfaction that the lady's son, who, unknown to the whole family, had entertained a passion for me, obtained his mother's leave to

B

marry me. As he had a great deal of good sense and
virtue, and was very agreeable in his person, I married
him. We did not live together above two years before he
died, leaving a beautiful daughter, and me mistress of a
large fortune. My patroness dying soon after, I came
over to England, together with my daughter, where I live
retired, busied only in the care of my Charlotte's education."

The merchant, who had listened with the greatest attention to this account which Miss Catley gave of herself,
admired her great virtue, wisdom and prudence. It gave
him infinite pleasure to find she was not married, and he
could not help expressing his joy to her on that account.
He then proceeded to make a formal declaration of his
love, but how much was be chagrined, when this lady of
pretended virtue, told him she was determined never to
marry a second time, and therefore begged him to relinquish
all thoughts of wedlock, as she had made a vow to remain
single during the rest of her life. She told him that she
should always rank him among her friends, and therefore
begged he would honour her so far as to place her among
the number of his. He politely thanked her and begged
to see her daughter. This request our heroine expected he
would make, and had accordingly procured a little girl
about seven years old, who was to pass as her daughter.
She rang the bell and ordered the maid to bring the child,
and presently after, a beautiful girl about seven years old,
richly dressed, entered the room. The supposed mother
presented her to Fernandes, who after having caressed her,
begged leave of Miss Catley to present her with what he
called an earnest of his future good intentions towards her.
Saying this, he put a pearl necklace into her hands and a

pair of ear rings mounted in gold, with diamond drops. These were delivered immediately to our heroine, who civilly thanked the gentleman for his ingenious present. After having drunk tea, he desired permission to retire, which having obtained, he went home, where we will leave him awhile to acquaint the reader with the reasons of Miss Catley's acting in the manner above related.

She always held it a duty incumbent on her to get all she could, without rendering herself too cheap ; she therefore always made it a rule to make her lovers pay exorbitantly for the smallest favours, and she was never known to complete anyone's happiness till she had gratified her passion for money. This mode of conduct, which she ever most religiously observed, has long since convinced the world, that, as Peachum's daughter in the *Beggar's Opera* says, " She knows as well how to make the most of her man as any woman." But in the present case she had other motives, though all had the same tendency, *i.e.* interest, for behaving as she did. She was now in keeping by Sir F. B. D., who rewarded her supposed constancy with too much liberality to suffer her to give him the least room to suspect her capable of being guilty of a breach of it.

On the other hand she seemed coy to her new lover, first, to prove the extent of his passion ; secondly, to raise in him a higher esteem for her ; and thirdly, to invent a scheme to prevent her two lovers from coming to the knowledge of her intimacy with either.

We will now return to Fernandes, who by this time was arrived at his own house. He went to bed much chagrined, but could not get a wink of sleep during the whole night. He lamented his unhappy fate in having met with so cruel a fair one. Having passed a sleepless night, in the morning he sent a servant with the following *billet*.

" Cruel Charmer !

How shall I find words to express the ardour of my passion for you, and lament the hardness of your heart in thus treating your humble slave ! Unless you relieve my pain, I shall inevitably fall a sacrifice to your beauty. I shall ever offer the incense of the purest praise of you at the altar of love. On your answer depends my life. If you continue to be cruel, I shall soon put an end to a wretched life.   I am yours,

M. D. FERNANDES."

To this passionate epistle our heroine returned the following answer.

" Sir,

I am not so cruel in my disposition as you imagine. I consent to alleviate your pain. I expect you this evening at my house. Come alone at seven o'clock.

P.S.—Let this be a profound secret.

A. C——Y."

Fernandes received this letter with joy, he kissed it a thousand times, and waiting with the utmost impatience for the appointed hour, which had no sooner come than he flew at once to meet his charmer whom he found in perfect readiness to meet him ; when he took his leave he was so satisfied with the reception that had been accorded him that he presented her with a note of a hundred pounds.

Whether Fernandes was not altogether quite as agreeable to Miss C——y as could have been expected, or whether for other more cogent reasons, she did not judge it prudent to encourage a renewal of his visits, cannot be ascertained. It is however certain that she never gave him the pleasure of her company after.

She continued to revel for a considerable time in all the pleasures which gallantry and dissipation afford, happy in the enjoyment of the affectionate indulgence shewn by her knight, till the golden stream of felicity was, for a short interval, turned into another channel, different from that in which it had so long run. This unexpected stroke of temporary unhappiness was occasioned by her father's taking upon him to vindicate the supposed injury done to his daughter's character by certain of these intimacies. He accordingly entered a process against Sir F. B. D., as principal agent, and also against B., the organist, for being an accomplice in the affair. The cause was tried at Westminster in 1764, when, it appearing to the judges that the knight's intimacy with our heroine was entirely with her own consent, and that Mr. B. could not in any manner be considered as an abettor or aider to the transaction, her indentures having been previously cancelled, her father, who doubtless expected to have gained considerably by the lawsuit, had the mortification to hear the jury pronounce a verdict for the defendant with costs of suit; which, as they were considerable, and out of the plaintiff's power to pay, the knight generously discharged.

This affair being thus settled, our heroine resumed her former gaiety, and shone with greater splendour than before at all places of polite resort. Her lover grew fonder of her every day, giving her frequent marks of his esteem. During the course of their intimacy, which lasted two years, two children were born, who both died in their infancy. They did not continue long together afterwards, an event happening which caused a final separation between them. It was as follows :

Miss C——y had been one evening at Vauxhall in

company with some ladies, from which place, filled with wine, a vice she was sometimes guilty of, she went with the rest of her company to W—th—by's, a well-known house of questionable repute, where she passed the night in mirth and jollity. Unluckily, Sir F. B. D. came there also, to pass an idle hour or two, and the waiter by mistake shewed him into an apartment where our heroine was in company with a young attorney's clerk. The indignant knight, fired with rage, turned on his heel and departed. The next morning she returned home, where she found her lover, who awaited her arrival. He reproached her for her baseness, as he termed it, towards him, and giving her a bank-note of £50 desired her to take another lodging immediately. Miss C——y, finding that all endeavours to please him were in vain, retorted his upbraidings on himself, and even went so far as to make herself merry at his expense.

It must not be supposed by the reader that the fault was all on one side, a mistake very often made with regard to affairs of this particular nature. In order therefore to do justice to all parties and that the true position of things may be understood it is necessary to insert the following.

Sir Francis Blake Delaval was a gentleman of high and respectable family, being son to a baronet and related nearly by blood and affinity to several of the nobility. His person was elegant, his face handsome, his manners polished, his education liberal, his conversation sprightly and pleasing. Few ever possessed so many of those qualities which fascinate the ladies, and few ever succeeded better in obtaining their favours by humbling their proud hearts. When very young this gentleman dissipated his patrimony on women and play, till at last his finances being reduced to the lowest ebb, necessity forced him to relieve them by fortune hunting, a resource truly despicable.

The object fixed upon as the means of repairing his shattered fortune, was Lady Isabella Pawlet, daughter to the Earl of Thanet. This lady possessed a very considerable fortune, with a very plain person and face, and a character somewhat questionable according to evidence said to be given by Foote, though unstained by any actual charges.

The truth is, Lady Isabella Pawlet (or Paulet) had a *penchant* for the humorist, and if he had not been restrained from matrimony, by having previously entered into the indissoluble noose of Hymen, there is scarcely a doubt that he would have refused the acceptance of a considerable fortune on any terms; but this being impossible, he resolved to come in for a share, and fixed upon Delaval, with whom he had long lived on terms of intimacy, as a proper instrument.

Lady Isabella was a dupe to superstition. The old gipsy woman at Norwood, whom she frequently visited, stood higher in her estimation than Boyle or Newton, and she put more confidence in the presages of an astrologer who resided up four pairs of stairs in the Old Bailey, than was ever placed in Copernicus.

Foote having informed his friend Delaval of the lady's foible, they came to an agreement, by which the former was to have an annuity of five hundred pounds a year, and the principal to enjoy the remainder of the lady's fortune.

A maid servant was bribed to betray her lady, and the conspirators having received information from her of a particular day when her ladyship was to consult a cele-brated conjuror, to whom, at that time, several women of the first fashion paid frequent visits, to this imposing rascal, Delaval and his friend Foote immediately repaired, and having secured his services by a few guineas, informed him of several of the most remarkable incidents in Lady Isabella's life, the conjuror at the same time taking an exact survey of Delaval's face and figure for a purpose which shall appear presently.

Lady Isabella soon after arrived, accompanied by her treacherous attendant, who by a sign previously agreed upon, informed the impostor who his visitor was.

The answers given to the interrogatories of her ladyship, and to the prepared questions occasionally slipped in by her cunning abigail, left no doubt on her mind of the conjuror's extraordinary and supernatural powers, and of course brought forward the material enquiry respecting marriage, which is generally the great end of all such applications.

The impostor now pretended to consult a planetary system that lay before him on his table. Having deliberately taken off a pair of large spectacles and turned up his eyes towards Heaven, he muttered over the names given to the signs of the zodiac and fixed stars,—he drew a number of circles and lines with white lead upon black paper, and at last with a grave face described the person and features of Delaval.

Lady Isabella, delighted at the description of her intended *cara sposa*, rewarded the conjuror liberally, and would now have retired, but her well-instructed companion, pretending a tender interest in the future fortune of her mistress, urged for further information, particularly as to the time when and the place where her lover was to be seen. The wizard answered that he could certainly com-

municate such information, but must first consult his
familiar spirit in an adjacent room, and immediately retired
to Delaval and Foote, who sat in another room, where
having waited a few minutes in consultation, he returned
to the women, and found Lady Isabella almost maddened
with anxious expectation. He told her that the gentleman
to whom the fates had destined her hand would be walking
the next day at twelve o'clock by the side of the canal in
the Green Park, but cautioned her not to speak first, as
that would break the charm, and having received another
fee for his pleasing news, Lady Isabella returned home in
rapture.

The description of the charming man described by the
conjuror had taken possession of this unfortunate lady's
brain; she could not eat during the day, nor sleep during
the night. The morning sun, on rising, found her at her
toilette, culling ornaments, painting, washing, and per-
fuming; and she involuntarily rambled to the place of
appointment an hour before the time. During this hour
this infatuated dupe to imposition kept her eyes rivetted
on the park gate, and every time it opened trembled from
head to foot with anxious expectation. Her repeater at
last struck twelve, and at that instant Delaval appeared,
dressed in every point exactly as the conjuror had described.

The sudden appearance of the gentleman extorted the
ejaculation of "O heavens!" from the lady, which was
followed with "Lord preserve us!" from the maid; but
Delaval continued to pass and repass them several times
without turning his eyes towards the seat, which was
indeed a necessary precaution, as he was ready to burst
into loud laughter every instant. At last, looking full at
Lady Isabella, he bowed respectfully, and, she returning

the salute, he walked towards her, and commenced a conversation.

The surprise of the lady having by degrees subsided, she discovered on recovering her senses that the stranger held her hand; she reluctantly drew it from him, at the same time heaving a deep sigh, which he returned with all the softness of sympathetic tenderness. Before they parted an assignation was made for a future meeting at the same place, and the swain took leave with an affected warmth of passion and respect that totally threw the lady off her guard, and expelled from her mind all considerations but those of romantic love.

Delaval, on separating, flew to inform Foote of his success, and then retired to indulge in tender conversation with a favourite in King's Place. Lady Isabella locked herself within her chamber, there to contemplate with rapture the conquest she had made, or rather, indeed, on the lover, who, in her opinion, Heaven in its bounty had created for her specially. The more she thought the more she became enamoured, and the second meeting totally overturned every idea that prudence suggested. Delaval

" ———— Could impart
The loosest wishes to the chastest heart."

And Lady Isabella was now at an age when the heart is tender, though not over young. She was approaching towards that grand climacteric which brings despair to maidens, and having long regretted her situation she was resolved not to lose the present opportunity of doing all within her power for the good of her generation, and to remove from herself that most horrid of all horrid epithets to a woman's ear—an old maid.

The marriage, therefore, was soon celebrated, much to the satisfaction of the bride ; but Sir Francis felt himself rather uneasy on the occasion, which, however, he attempted to put off with a laugh, and having been asked how he could think of marrying so ordinary a woman, answered "I married her for weight and paid nothing for fashion."

Had Lady Isabella been a Venus in beauty, and endowed with the wisdom of Pallas, she would have found her charms of body and mind unequal to fix the heart of Delaval, ever on search for variety, and never satisfied with any single object. But in truth her ladyship was destitute not only of personal charms but of mental allurements—her conversation was as plain as her face.

A young lady named Roche lived at this time under the protection of a near female relative to Delaval, and was supposed by many to be a natural daughter to one of the family. In the leading astray of this girl he soon succeeded. Her mind was weak, her constitution meretricious, and instead of retreating from him, and repelling his overtures, she met his affections with ardour, and lived with him as his mistress for a considerable time—indeed it was a doubtful point which of the two was most in the wrong.

This inconstancy on the part of Delaval naturally excited resentment in the lady. Female pride could not patiently submit to so gross an insult. She saw her fortune bestowed upon a courtesan ; she felt that the husband to whom she had administered the means of indulging his pleasures affronted her by publicly appearing and living with his mistress, and privately treating her, his wife, with neglect, and even contempt that evinced disgust. This roused her to revenge. She upbraided her husband with bitterness,

he answered with cutting coolness, and in the height of one
of their disputes discovered the secret of the conjuror.

Lady Isabella consulted her friends on this occasion and
they brought in the aid of the law.   A case was drawn
and a suit of divorce was determined on, upon the grounds
that Delaval had committed adultery with Miss Roche.
Of the truth of this charge there could not be a doubt, but
Lady Isabella failed in the proof.   The witnesses gave
evidence of the parties having rode out together, having
dined together, having lodged in the same house together,
but they failed in legally proving the offence on the
ground of which she sought relief and release from her
marriage contract.

Delaval thinking he had no offence to make, resolved
upon obviating the effect of his wife's complaint, which if
established would have materially injured his fortune, and
therefore he set up a charge of recrimination.

This charge states that a person named Craig took a
woman with him to Haddock's, at Charing Cross, on the
evening of a day when Delaval had invited some company
to meet him at the Cardigan's Head Tavern, Charing Cross,
among whom was the late Mr. Robert Quaime.   To this
company he communicated that he had long believed his
wife to be inconstant, and had received information that
she was to be that night at Haddock's with a man who
went by the name of Brown, that he intended to be
convinced of the truth, and requested that the company
would go to the house with him in order to see if they
could detect her in the act.   One Dupree was then despatched to Haddock's, and soon sent back a messenger to
inform Delaval that his wife was arrived.   The company
then went to the place, when Dupree opened the door of a

room where Lady Isabella was said to be, and where they saw a man and woman, the latter of whom one of the witnesses swore was Lady Isabella, but in this he was not corroborated by any of the other witnesses.

It was also deposed that her ladyship passed by the name of Brown and met Craig, who also assumed that name, at a lodging in Beaufort Buildings, where they passed for man and wife ; but the general opinion was, that the whole of the evidence against Lady Isabella was fabricated and false and that her witnesses had been tampered with and suborned. This suit in the commons of course terminated all connubial connection between Delaval and his wife, nor did his intimacy with Miss Roche continue much longer.

As there is something particular and interesting in the story of this lady, though it is not immediately connected with the memoirs of Nan, yet the reader will find entertainment from the perusal.

Sir Henry Echlin an Irish baronet, who possessed a very considerable estate at Rush, near Dublin, having seen Miss Roche became enamoured of her beauty, and indeed it must be allowed her charms were attractive.

Sir Henry was a young man of very weak intellect in worldly matters, extremely dissipated, naturally extravagant and totally devoid of foresight.

He had been a dupe to gamblers, money lenders, bullying captains, the keepers of low houses, &c., and yet he was a man of liberal education, elegant address and master of all the polite languages. Probably he winked at the *faux-pas* imputed by public report to Miss Roche, who conducted herself with such cunning that his addresses terminated in a marriage.

Sir Henry soon after this happy event returned to his native country, accompanied by his lady and a gentleman who lived with him as a confidential friend. On this journey Lady Echlin, who delighted in variety, was improperly intimate with the friend of her husband, making him dupe to her own disgrace, and he was the only person of a large company who travelled with them, who did not see the gross conduct of his wife.

Soon after their arrival in Ireland this intrigue came glaring in his face, and had he permitted his wife to live with him every boy would have hooted him—no legal steps however were taken in consequence of her conduct, but they separated by mutual consent; Sir Henry remaining at his country seat, and his lady removing to elegant lodgings in Capel Street, Dublin.

In this situation Lady Echlin gave way completely to that immoral disposition and habit that had long characterised her, and among other degrading connections formed one with the son of an attorney, a stupid creature destitute of every quality that was not merely animal. Another and another soon succeeded—man was her object, sensuality her pursuit—"every rank fool went down." A conduct so obnoxious, so foreign to the delicacy of her sex, soon reduced her to a state of contempt. Wherever she appeared the women retreated, and even the men were ashamed to shew her countenance in public. This marked, yet just punishment of her offences, rendered Dublin a solitude— she found herself without society, and daily experienced insult, to avoid which she made a trip to London. This was only changing the scene. In London her pursuits were the same as in Dublin, and it is generally believed that in a few years after she died miserably in the garret of a wretched lodging house in one of the alleys of Drury Lane.

The pursuits of Sir Henry were not more reputable than those of his lady ; his house exhibited a scene of continued revelling, debauchery and extravagance—mortgage followed mortgage—foreclosures produced sales, till at last the unhappy baronet was obliged to fly his country and was so reduced in circumstances, that he officiated at Paris in the degrading situation of a waiter. Afterwards, however, he emerged from that degenerate situation, and received a trifling pension for the performance of secret services.

After Miss Catley's quarrel with Sir Francis, and their separation, she removed to a milliner's shop in Tavistock-street, Covent Garden, which situation was the more agreeable to her, as being highly convenient for the business she carried on. It must however be remarked that this fall from greatness was highly disgusting to a person of our heroine's disposition. She was naturally fond of splendour, and having been accustomed to parade the streets in her chariot could hardly support the thought of walking on foot. Being a woman of spirit her change of circumstance did not affect her so much as it would have done others. She resolved to cast her eye about for another lover to supply the place of her former one.

A female performer no sooner starts in a line like this, if she is only tolerably handsome and has any degree of merit in her profession, than she has a number of professed admirers. It is the ambition of every pretty fellow to aim at being the happy man, and an artful girl acquainted with the wiles of her class, in such a situation, cannot fail of attracting a great many lovers. Our heroine's

talents and beauty were so superior to most contemporaries
in her profession, that the reader need not be surprised to
find her particularly distinguished ; and that the number
of her admirers were in proportion.   She had indeed many,
both in England and Ireland, as will be seen in the course of
this work.   We may venture to assert, that there never
perhaps was a more sincere devotee to the goddess of love
than this lady, nor one who has made a better use of the
vast sums she has acquired in her profession, in which
she has not only the greatest share of pleasure, but has
also reaped immense profits.   She was engaged at Covent
Garden Theatre at this time, where her salary indeed was
but moderate, but which, however, united to the returns of
her other business, placed her in a state of affluence.   Add
to this what she gained by singing at private concerts
during the winter season, and her lucrative appointment at
Marylebone Gardens in the summer time, then under the
direction of that arch-priest of Salinus, Tom L—— of
intriguing memory.

As we have stated, soon after her quarrel with Delaval,
Anne, acting under advice she respected, made a trip to
Ireland.   Her reception in the "land of saints," fully
answered her most sanguine expectations ; she drew over-
flowing audiences, who applauded her to "the very echo,"
and raised considerable sums for herself and the manager.
In Dublin, however, a circumstance occurred which for a
time considerably damped her spirits, and mortified her
pride.   Nan was not an only child ; she had a sister named
Mary, whom she took into the family, for the purpose of
superintending two children, one of whom she taught to
call Sir Francis Delaval father, the other she honoured
with royal blood, named him Edward, and gave him for
a sire his Royal Highness the late Duke of York.

It must be acknowledged by Nan's best friends that she did not behave affectionately to her sister Poll. The girl was kept at a distance, treated as a servant, and, as Nan's disposition often broke out with all the unbounded virulence of a vulgar termagant, the poor creature suffered not only from the abuse of her tongue, which was pointed and poisoned like that of an asp, but also from the violence of her fists, and sharpness of her nails, which she could exercise with such agility and effect that a black eye, or bloody nose and cheeks were frequently the consequence.

This ill usage, which was almost daily repeated, determined poor Poll to quit her sister. She had a good voice, though uncultivated, a small, neat, smart person, and good eyes; but the smallpox had ravaged the charms of her face, which, however, displayed the lily and the rose, so that she was desirable, though not beautiful, and had many admirers. One of these laid close siege to Poll, who for a considerable time rejected his addresses. Wearied out, however, at last, by the repeated ill-usage of her tyrannical sister, who rendered home a hell, she flew to the protection of her lover.

The rage of Nan on this occasion is not easily described; cups, saucers, every article at hand, flew about the house; she felt for the honour of her family, and a violent fit of hysterics was the consequence. Recovering from this paroxysm of rage and pride, she became calm and vindictive; and having relieved her oppressed mind by a shower of tears, and a torrent of abuse against the cause of her grief, made a positive vow never to see or relieve her runaway sister, which vow she kept most religiously.

Poll's charms, as has been already hinted at, were not very fascinating, and her lover soon became disgusted with

C

his mistress, whom he one day caught intriguing with a student of Dublin College, and of course dismissed her on this positive proof of unfaithfulness.

Poll's new lover, the collegian, though rich in learning was poor in purse; but he was young and agreeable, qualities of high estimation with every female, and which had such effect upon this lady that, notwithstanding several overtures had been made, she rejected them all, and for near six months lived, or rather starved, in fidelity with the man of letters. "Love," says the old proverb, "flies out of the window when poverty enters the door." The adage, however, was not illustrated by the conduct of Poll, who, for a considerable time after poverty had taken possession of her apartment, worked to supply the wants of her favourite swain. The student was seized with a severe illness, which, baffling all the efforts of the physicians, assumed the form of a decline, and in the end caused his death. Poll, too, was laid up in hospital for a considerable time, but ultimately recovered; and, having a tolerable voice, and a name which would make an attractive figure in a country playbill, got an engagement in a strolling company, from which time fame has neglected to report the incidents of her life.

In Ireland it is certain that Nan had many intrigues, in most of which she acted with caution and prudence. Such as had merely pleasure in view were mostly confined to the gentlemen of the sock and buskin; with the great, profit was always her object, and secresy a part of the condition she imposed upon her lovers. Being herself independent of the world, and freed from every species of control, her amours offered no variety of incident. By this means, and the profits of her profession, Nan's finances

increased considerably, and she prudently secured and
increased them, always living much below her income.
There never was a greater favourite in Dublin, nor
indeed a more deserving one, for on every opportunity
she obliged the public, and by them was constantly
rewarded at her benefits.

She was perhaps the only woman leading such a life that
ever received countenance on the stage from the modest
women of Ireland; but they looked upon her as an
eccentric character, making proper allowances for her early
habits, and imputed her failings more to early misfortune
than to vice.

At this time the reverend Dean Bailey was a principal
superintendent to most of the public charities, and it having
been determined that a concert should be performed for the
benefit of the lying-in hospital, the dean, who was particularly attentive to this charity, took upon him to
engage Catley to sing at the concert, and wrote her a card
to the following purport. " Dean Bailey's compliments to
Miss Catley, and requests to know when she can give him
a night at the lying-in hospital, and her terms."   On this
card Nan put a jocular interpretation, and returned for
answer, " Miss Catley presents her compliments to the
Reverend Dean Bailey ; for three nights to come she is
engaged to particular friends, but on the fourth will be
at his service." This produced a laugh against the Dean,
but in the end served the charity, for which Nan sung
gratis.

The world has often heard of Lord R——— who some
years ago was tried at the Quarter Sessions at Dublin,
upon a charge, which if true, would have been the most
disgraceful to him, as it is disgusting and shocking to

mankind. The manners of this nobleman abounded with peculiarities. He was tall and bony in person, yet effeminate in every action ; with a skin tawny as a mulatto, and a beard thick, strong and black as that of a Swiss ; he affected the delicacy and nervous sensations of a sickly girl. Some ill demon put it into his lordship's head to have an affair with Miss Catley ; probably for the purpose of lessening the effect of several evil suspicions which then flew about, materially to the injury of his character, in respect to the affection of his passions.

The noble lord had not at this time attained the considerable estates which he afterwards inherited from his father ; and which might have accounted for the economic plan by which he approached Miss Catley, if it was not known that even then he abounded in wealth, and that parsimony was among his faults. He waited on Nan one evening soon after she had returned from performing Captain Flash in the Farce of *Miss in her Teens*, in which character, the appearance being masculine, for Nan was then an excellent breeches figure, she had struck his eye, and raised ideas very difficult for persons of his lordship's taste to suppress.

Nan on her return had sat down to prepare supper for a few theatrical friends whom she intended to treat with a roast duck and having recently parted with her servant, was officiating as cook at her chamber fire, where the duck hung pendant from a string.

His lordship having been announced by the landlady, was ordered to be ushered in. In a few complimentary excuses, he apologised for so abrupt a visit, declared his passion was pure and disinterested and regretted in very pointed terms that so fine a shape should be concealed by

petticoats. Nan received his address with affected com-
plaisance and satisfaction ; swore that had she expected
the pleasure of his lordship's company, he should not have
found her in dishabille, and pressed him to do her the honour
of picking the breast of the bird that was then roasting.
Nothing could be more agreeable to his lordship's disposition than this invitation. He praised Catley for her
economy in doing her own business, and then he praised
the duck. She turned the string, he handed the dredging
box—never was lord more happy, till in the midst of his
culinary offices, a knocking at the door gave an alarm.
Nan was then in lodgings, with the exclusive privilege of
monopolizing the hall door to her own use. " It must be
some person for me," said Nan, "for heaven's sake, my lord,
turn the duck while I run to the door." His lordship
obeyed and placing himself upon a little stool, which Nan
had occupied by the fire-side, commenced his new profession
of cook with extraordinary satisfaction and adroitness.

Nan's theatrical friends, for it was they who were at the
door, having been conducted into the drawing room, where
the cloth was laid, she welcomed them with an assurance
that the supper she had provided was not only good but
had been dressed by one of the first cooks in Europe, and
opening the door suddenly introduced the astonished lord
to their wondering eyes.

" Take care cooky, said Nan " if the duck be burned, I
shall certainly discharge you from your place.

The degenerate nobleman felt to the very soul the con-
temptible situation to which his passion for a fine figure
had reduced him.   He arose from the stool overwhelmed
with confusion ; his dress was brown velvet embroidered
with gold, point ruffles and a bag, at his side hung a sword

and elegant knot, in his hand he held a basting ladle dropping butter.

Fancy may easily paint his lordship's figure on her tablets; but to give the true delineation and *contour* of humour to the eye, requires the execution of a Hogarth or a Bunbury. It was nature metamorphosed, by the workings of shame and surprise, into the most extravagant contortions of caricature. Nor were the painters, the engravers, or the poets idle on the subject; his lordship was sketched in aquafortis, stuck up in every print shop and lampooned in every newspaper.

Another adventure which took place nearly at the same period as the foregoing, does equal credit to Nan's humour and understanding. She had long been an object of attention to an old and dissipated rake following the wine business, by whom she had been very much annoyed. This fellow in appearance and mind was the perfect representative of a satyr, he was completely worn out with debauchery and dissipation, yet, notwithstanding his ugliness and debility, was inflated with vanity to an enormous extent and imputed to the influence of his address, person, and conversation the success and attachments which resulted solely from the power of his money, or rather indeed the money of his creditors, which he squandered in a most shameful manner, though husband to an amiable wife and father of several children.

Nan having repelled all his efforts successfully, he resolved to attack her gratitude by paying tribute to her avarice, and for this purpose sent a *billet-doux* requesting an appointment to supper and with it a large hamper of champagne, assuring her that the cellar it came from was at her service, and afforded as great a variety as France, Spain, Portugal, or Italy could supply. The wine was received, and a verbal message of thanks returned, but the very same evening it was sent back to the merchant's house with a card directed to his wife informing her of the fact.

At supper the wife declared she had a longing for champagne and must have a glass. The husband stared and railed at her extravagance. " But I will treat you, my dear," said the wife, " you may see I have received a present," on which she put Catley's note into his hands. It is easy to conceive the domestic quarrel that ensued, and the person here alluded to has for years back lived in London in the most indigent circumstances.

It has already been observed that Miss Catley was avaricious, yet she had her favourites who succeeded in duping her even out of her money, as for instance in the case of Major F—m—g. Her connection with this man, who was aide-de-camp to the Lord Lieutenant of Ireland when she resided in that kingdom, was by no means advantageous. The major was penurious, not only from disposition but necessity, and Nan shared with him not only her favours but her purse. With Captain C——e, who succeeded the major, she was equally infatuated, and yet never did nature produce a stronger contrast between two men. F——g, was tall, strong, and manly. Clarke was not above the middle size, weak and effeminate, he patched and painted like a woman, and, in appearance, bore a stronger resemblance to an eunuch than to a man. Yet to this insect was Catley attached, on this insect she bestowed considerable sums, though she used frequently, and even in his presence, to rally her own choice, declaring that he was in no respect suited to a woman of spirit and gallantry.

From the fascinating spell with which this *petit maitre*

trammelled the affections of Nan she was freed by the exorcisms of General Lascelles, then only a captain in the army.

One very peculiar attachment she formed was to Mr. P——, and this deserves to be noticed among the various oddities of the age. He was possessed of near three hundred pounds a year, of which he did not save a farthing though a bachelor, and a parsimonious man to all outward appearance. He was neither a patriot nor a ministerial advocate. His sentiments in politics indeed he had never revealed, but from the tenor of his whole conduct he seemed not to care a farthing which courtier enjoyed the post of prime minister. It was extremely difficult to form a just idea of his sentiments upon any subject whatever, as he seldom spoke unless it was to ask for the necessaries of life.

He took up his lodgings at an inn in the city in which he resided several years. For the first six months he frequently went to a very noted and genteel public-house, being a great admirer of fine ale, but having an utter aversion to the trouble of dress, and having a particular attachment to one shirt for a number of weeks, it was hinted to him by the master of the house how necessary it would be to clean himself if he proposed resorting thither, as the other gentlemen were offended at his appearance.

Mr. P—— was affronted at this insinuation, and showed his resentment by never going thither afterwards, for considering his shirt as the nearest thing to him in the world he resolved not to part with it as long as it would stick by him. For this reason he was confined to his hotel, where he admitted no one into his room, making his own bed, if ever it was made, and doing everything for himself. For fear of being robbed, imitating thereby the French poet, who

threw his money among his faggots, Mr. P—— upon the
receipt of a sum used to give it a jerk under the bed, and
as long as he could find a single guinea without trouble, he
never thought of a clean shirt or the bank. He was, however, once, unfortunately, reduced to his last moidore, and
arrived at the *ne plus ultra* of filth and rags, and must
have been reduced to the mortifying necessity of changing
his linen, pulling up the heels of his shoes thereby to
conceal the holes in his stockings, which were at that time
very conspicuous, in order to repair to the bank to receive
his last half-year's interest, which always lay dormant till
he was in the greatest distress.

Mr. P—— was not without vices. Though ostentation
and ambition were not among the number ; he was a great
votary of Bacchus, to whom he devoted not only his nights
and days but also his fortune. Loquacity he contemned,
reason he despised, dress he set at naught, women he was
once passionately fond of, but at the time we are speaking
of, they, Miss Catley excepted, had no charms. But his
jolly god was his constant friend and advocate, with him
alone he used to confer, and he seemed resolved to live
and die in such celestial company. He once obtained a
temporary relief from a disagreeable necessity of going out,
through the industry of an army of moths who had eaten
the lining of an old waistcoat in which were concealed near
thirty guineas and which was going to be thrown upon the
dunghill.

With this charming Adonis did our heroine pass away
now and then a leisure hour, and she would probably have
liked him well enough had he been cleanly. Neatness of
dress she always admired, no wonder then if his excessive
passion for slovenliness disgusted her, and obliged her to

quit the society of such a man to enjoy the more refined
delights that resulted from the engaging conversation of
Lord B———t, with whom she had at this time contracted a
close intimacy, and who gratified every wish she could form
with the greatest generosity.   He had seen her perform on
the stage, was charmed with her and took her home in his
chariot, hired an elegant house for her and maintained her
in the greatest splendour.

  Of all the connections formed by Miss Catley, perhaps
the one that ultimately exercised the greatest and most
beneficial influence over her life was that with the General
Lascelles already briefly alluded to; indeed, when her
relationship with this gentleman was settled by her marriage,
it seemed to mark the real turning point of her life.   It
appears that the gallant officer, who in 1768 was promoted
to the rank of a lieutenant-colonel of dragoons, went over
to Ireland about that date to join his regiment which
lay in the city of Dublin.   Miss Catley had been in that
metropolis three years, in consequence of her having made
an engagement with Mr. Mossop to perform at the theatre,
and where she had been received with almost universal and
justly merited applause, particularly as a vocal performer.
It may easily be supposed that she was no less than a reign-
ing toast in that great city, where the queen of love held as
extensive an empire as in the English metropolis.   Colonel
Lascelles went to the play one evening, and having seen our
heroine perform the part of Rosetta, was smitten with love
of her.   He accordingly soon got introduced to her behind
the scenes, and the great politeness, refined sense, and un-
wearied assiduity to please her, joined to his personal
recommendations, which were the strongest imaginable and
sufficient to have captivated a heart less susceptible of love

than Miss C——y's, distinguished him from the herd of her
admirers, and she almost as speedily convinced the world
how greatly she was prejudiced in his favour by the
partiality she testified for him, in consenting to live with
him, preferably to any other of her lovers. Before entering
at any length upon this connection, which leads to the
closing scenes of her life, there are two or three other
matters necessary to be narrated in order to make the story
complete.

One of her most conspicuous intrigues was with a silk
mercer, Mr. S——t, who lived near Fleet Street.   The
manner of their first acquaintance was truly romantic, as
follows :—

She was going home one evening from the play, and, it
being moonlight and a frost, she chose to walk rather than
ride in a chair.   As she was crossing over the end of James
Street, she perceived a young man before her, who by his
appearance seemed to be very well in his circumstances.
Being now entirely destitute of a keeper, she determined to
throw out a lure to attract his notice. She accordingly had
scarcely reached the opposite footpath when, pretending to
stumble, she caught hold of the skirt of his coat in order to
save herself.   He immediately stretched out his hand to
raise her up, and begged to have the honour of being
permitted to wait on her to her lodgings. The kind fair
one, overjoyed at this opportunity which fortune had thrown
in her way, consented, though with some seeming reluctance.
Having escorted her home, he took his leave of her in the
politest manner imaginable, and begged she would not think
him guilty of too much presumption on her goodness if he
should take the liberty of enquiring after her health.   She
gave him a suitable answer and they parted.

The smitten silk-man paid her a visit the next day about twelve o'clock and was received with much decorum. She did not offer to impose on him a well invented tale, as she had done on the Jew merchant. Her appearance, everything about her, the very house she lived in proclaimed her a lady of easy virtue. Such a one her new acquaintance wished her to be, and he made no scruple of making her an advantageous proposal that very hour, which she thought proper to accept, and from that day commenced an intimacy between them.

He was a man who had seen more of the world than the generality of people in his sphere of life are supposed to do. He had fine parts well cultivated by a good education, and a large share of experience of mankind. He was of a generous disposition, and susceptible of the most tender passions, particularly that which the little god Cupid inspires. No wonder therefore if Miss Catley appeared so charming in his eyes. His heart had imbibed a passion, which nothing, to all appearance, could ever eradicate. Unfortunately he was married to a very virtuous and beautiful woman, who had brought him two fine children, a boy and a girl.

Notwithstanding all his allurements to love his own family alone, he became so infatuated with the charms of his new mistress, that forgetful of the ties of nature, he attached himself entirely to her.

The better to carry on this intrigue, 'twas agreed between them, that our heroine should become a customer of the shop, and as such, frequently go thither under pretence of buying goods : but in reality to take off all suspicion of any criminal intercourse between them. The mercer took his leave, slipping a £20 note into her hands, and she promised to go next day to his house to look at some new fashioned silks that were just made up purposely for the spring wear.

She did not fail to go the next forenoon according to the appointment with Mr. S——t, and was introduced into the parlour behind the shop, by his wife, who not knowing her character, treated her with all the good manners she was mistress of. After having looked over a large quantity of different patterns, she ordered some of those which she liked best to be sent home to her lodgings, and was about to take her leave which she was prevented from doing by the mercer and his wife, who both pressed her in the most obliging manner imaginable, to stay and drink tea with them. She consented after much entreaty; which being over, she went away, her lover slipping a note into her hand at parting.

Eager to know the contents of the *billet*, as soon as she reached her lodgings, she opened it and read the following words.

" Dear Charmer,

The infinite pleasure your sweet company gave me this afternoon has by far overpaid me for the trifling things you had out of my shop ; I therefore beg of you to accept of them as a token of my love. My wife is immoderately fond of you and wishes for the pleasure of seeing you often. By compliance with her request, you will oblige me beyond expression, as you thereby afford me an opportunity of enjoying the sweets of your angelic conversation.   I am, loveliest of your sex,

Your sincere admirer

W. S——t."

Two days after Miss C——y received a visit from the enamoured mercer, who brought her a present of a beautiful set of Dresden china, and some of the finest tea that could be purchased. They made themselves very merry at his wife's credulity and passed the time in a most agreeable manner till it was time for him, that he might not give Mrs. S——t any cause of suspicion, to return home, which he did with the utmost reluctance.

Their intrigue did not (happily for the mercer) last above six months. During this short period, our heroine had cost him about five hundred pounds in presents of different kinds, including her weekly allowance of five guineas. An accident, however, happened, which terminated their guilty intercourse, occasioned by the mercer's being arrested for a large sum, and was as follows.

The reader need not be told that it is no uncommon thing for men in a large and extensive way of trade to be obliged to give very long credit, and that they sometimes meet with heavy losses. This was exactly the case of Mr. S——t, who, in making up great payments, had offered several notes and bills which he had received as money, and by the drawers he was forced either to take up himself, or be liable to be sent to prison for the sum of two thousand pounds, which was demanded of him at that time, and being unable to answer it, he was arrested and carried to the King's Bench, to the no small grief of his affectionate wife and family.

Our heroine who was totally ignorant of the affair, accidentally called at his shop the very day this misfortune happened, and, seeing Mrs. S——t in tears, earnestly desired to know the cause of her grief. The mercer's wife told her and Miss Catley cried out "O my dear Mr.

S——t !" She could say no more, but swooned. Mrs.
S——t, astonished at her behaviour, as soon as she was a
little recovered asked her what had caused such an emotion,
but our heroine, unable to answer her question properly,
only replied, " that the compassion she felt for Mr. S——t
on this melancholy occasion had caused her present illness."
Having said this, she desired a chair might be called, into
which she got and was carried home immediately.

Mrs. S——t went to her husband directly, and related
to him every circumstance of Miss Catley's behaviour. Her
narration filled him with the utmost confusion, from which
being somewhat recovered, he threw himself on his knees
before her, and gave her a circumstantial account of the
infamous connection that had so long subsisted between
him and the object of his lawless flame.

He was often interrupted by sighs and tears during
the melancholy relation of his former vices. His wife
wept bitterly over his past misconduct, but at the same
time was greatly comforted at the signs he gave of the
most genuine repentance. Heaven itself was also pleased
to approve his reformation and to reward it.

He that day received a letter, acquainting him that his
elder brother was dead in Bengal, and left him master of
a very ample fortune, and the same post which brought
him this welcome news, brought him also bills of exchange
payable at sight to the amount of upwards of £30,000.

He was immediately released from confinement, and
returned home to his own house. He left off trade as soon
as he conveniently could, and bought a large estate in the
country, to which place he removed his family, where he
now lives in the sweet society of his virtuous wife and
amiable offspring ; he adoring the kind interposition of

providence, which had thus miraculously snatched him from inevitable ruin, and she blessing his return to goodness, and offering up her daily prayers at the throne of grace for the prolongation of his life.

We now proceed to the relation of an adventure which she had with an old gentleman, a widower, who lived at Epsom, for the better understanding of which it will be proper to speak in this place, first, of her amour with his son, who was at that time a student in the university of Oxford. This young gentleman, after the example of most of the Oxonians, being tired of the vigorous discipline of the college, would, at certain intervals, make little excursions to London, in order to unbend his mind by partaking of the amusements that great metropolis afforded. In one of these journeys chance directed him to the theatre, where our heroine's voice so enchanted him that as soon as the play was over he enquired who she was and where she lived, and paid her a visit next morning.

Miss C——y was struck at the first sight with his genteel mien and address, and, considering him as a pretty fellow with whom she could pass away her leisure hours agreeably, she leaped into his embraces without the least hesitation. They saw each other frequently during his stay in London, which lasted about a fortnight, and on parting he presented her with a purse of gold.

The reader will please to take notice that he went by the name of H———s, though his real name was B———te.

To return to her intrigue with the old gentleman. She had been to Epsom to see an acquaintance, a lady who had retired on an easy fortune to the village already mentioned, where her remains of beauty had wrought so powerfully on the affections of a barrister-at-law that he had married her.

Old Mr. B———te used to visit at the house, and had frequent opportunities of seeing our heroine there. He was struck with her charms, perceiving which she resolved to try what effect her voice would have on him. She knew he was rich, and would therefore have gladly drawn him in for a husband. Accordingly, one afternoon, when he went to the house of Mrs. M———, he found her playing on the harpsichord and singing an Italian air. Highly delighted with the melody of her pipe, he desired her to repeat her song, which request she as obligingly complied with.

When she had done he passed the highest praises on her musical talents, and expressed a desire that she would undertake to teach his daughter, a girl of about fourteen years of age, to sing. Nan, who desired above all things an opportunity of introducing herself into his house, readily consented, promising to attend the young lady as often as business or pleasure should draw her into the country. She was as good as her word, and after the time of her visit to her friend at Epsom had expired she constantly went thither three times a week from London.

She found means to steal so far into the good graces of the whole family that the old gentleman's esteem for her ripened by degrees into a confirmed passion. He was, however, willing to try her some time longer before he made a formal declaration of love. She continued to do all in her power to please him, and was so punctual in her assiduities that he could no longer resist the impulse of his heart, which, with uninterrupted emotions, incited him in the strongest manner possible to make a formal profession of his flame. He did so, and had the happiness, as he esteemed it, to find that his suit met with a favourable reception. Our heroine could not have refused so advan-

D

tageous an offer without being guilty of the greatest folly imaginable. But that she might reap as much profit as ever she could from this union she told him that, previous to her giving him her hand in marriage, she insisted on his signing a paper, properly drawn up by an attorney, to screen her from any insults which might be offered her by his children, in case she should survive him, after his decease. This he readily agreed to, and the conditions were as follows :

First, that he should settle a thousand pounds on her, to be paid within one month after his funeral, and one hundred pounds a year during her natural life.

Secondly, that he should settle the like annuity on every one of the children she might have by him, to be paid them also during the term of their natural lives.

Thirdly, that previous to their marriage he should vest a sum or sums sufficient to produce the aforesaid annuities in any of the public funds, or lend the same on mortgages, on lands or houses, or on eligible securities, for the payment of them.

Fourthly, that in case of failure in any of the said conditions the marriage shall be null and void, and she shall be at liberty to marry again.

These conditions, however extravagant they may appear to the reader, he readily complied with, and the writings were accordingly drawn up with all convenient expedition, and signed by him in the presence of several witnesses. Preparations were now made for the nuptials with all imaginable haste, a new equipage was bespoke, an additional train of servants was hired, the wedding clothes were ordered, the ring was bought, the license was procured, and everything seemed to concur in making our heroine the

happiest of women, when an accident intervened which put
an end to her approaching felicity. The old gentleman
wrote a letter to his son, acquainting him with his intended
wedding, and demanding to see him immediately. The
young student hastened to London directly on the receipt
of his father's epistle, and arrived at his house the very
next day.

As soon as he came he was introduced to his intended
mother-in-law, but who can describe the amazement which
appeared in their countenances when they saw each other!
Old Mr. B——te, surprised at this extraordinary behaviour,
hastily enquired into the reason of it. His son for some
time could not utter a word, but at length, resuming his
courage, he fell on his knees and spoke as follows:

"Your pardon, honoured sir, for what I am going to
acquaint you with. About two months since, unknown to
you or any of my friends, I left the college and took a
journey to London. In the course of my rambles I made
acquaintance with this infamous woman, whom, to the
eternal disgrace of your family, you are going to raise to
the dignity of being your wife. I have seen my folly, and
promise in the sincerest manner possible never to be guilty
of the like again, provided you have the goodness to pardon
this slip of youth; and I flatter myself that which has been
the happy means of rescuing my family from dishonour will
contribute somewhat towards effecting a reconciliation with
you."

His father kept a profound silence all the while he was
talking, and for some minutes after. When he had done
speaking he made him a sign to follow him into his
closet, when having shut the door, he ordered him to relate
in the most circumstantial manner possible the whole

series of his adventures with Miss Catley. Young B——te
obeyed and his father forgave him, overjoyed at this lucky
discovery. He then returned to the parlour where he left
our heroine, and told her that he had been happy in finding
out what sort of a woman she was, before it was too late,
and therefore desired her to go away immediately. She did
not hesitate to comply with his request, and mounted a
chaise which conveyed her to her lodgings in town.

The following may be cited as an example of that
avariciousness of spirit which has been said to have distinguished this woman. In 1771, soon after her return to
England, a singing performer belonging to Covent Garden
Theatre, Mr. D——l—my, had obtained permission from the
Lord Chamberlain to have a play acted for his benefit
at the Haymarket play-house. Thinking our heroine's
appearance might be a means of drawing a crowded
audience, he waited on Miss C——y to be informed on
what terms she would represent her celebrated character of
Rosetta. She demanded the sum of forty guineas, but was
told that her price was too extravagant. She answered she
would not play for less money. He expostulated in the
strongest terms with her on the exorbitancy of her
demands, and succeeded so far as to obtain a promise from
her of playing for twenty. He issued his tickets, and
caused bills to be printed in which was her name. The
time now drew near for the fulfilling her engagement, when
she gave a signal proof of her avarice ; the night before the
representation, she sent him a card acquainting him that
she was taken suddenly ill, and could not possibly perform
the next evening. He plainly discovered the meaning of
the message and went to her. He represented the great
inconveniency a disappointment of this nature would

subject him to, and entreated her in the warmest manner to oblige him with her appearance on the promised night. She at last told him that unless he would give her thirty guineas, she would not perform. He complied and lost by his benefit.

Her engagement at Covent Garden Theatre, the ensuing season, was purely accidental. Mrs. Pinto had given notice to the managers that she would not renew her engagement for any longer time, as they refused to come to her terms, *i.e.* twenty guineas per week. They were therefore at a loss to find a proper woman to supply her place, and accordingly cast their eyes on our heroine; Mr. C——n was deputed by his colleagues to treat with her, and easily complied with her demands of fifteen guineas per week. She appeared soon after in public, and for the two first nights brought amazing great houses. But the company after this time began to decrease, and she received a second visit from Mr. C——n, who acquainted her that he, unknown to his brother managers, had agreed to give her her price, but that as the success had not answered their expectations, they could not think of paying her so extravagant a salary. To this harangue she returned the following answer. " Sir, I thought you were the sole acting manager, or else your law-suit has been decided to very little purpose ; however, my engagements were with you, and I expect you will fulfil them."

Saying this, she turned out of the room, singing the air of the last new birthday minuet.

She had long desired to be connected with Mr. Th—l—w the S—l—tor G—r—l, but was disappointed ; that gentleman, being already provided with a favourite, did not choose to enter into an intimacy with her. He, however, paid her

some occasional visits, which would have paved the way to
a further correspondence, had he not, unfortunatoly for her,
found her one morning, when he went to her lodgings,
with a silk mercer's clerk, who occasionally visited her.
Their intimacy accordingly broke off, and he never visited
her any more.

To return to Colonel Lascelles : We have already observed
that his fortune was but small, too small for the complexion
of his unbounded wishes. Notwithstanding the disagreeable, as well as involuntary indigence to which he was often
reduced, he always found means to render himself agreeable
to the fair sex, to whom he was so lavish in his adorations,
by his genteel air and engaging deportment, which was ever
such as could not fail to captivate the hearts of all those
with whom he conversed, particularly such as, unmindful of
the more refined and superior excellent interior accomplishments, are attached in a more peculiar manner to those of
the outside. His connection with our heroine had, besides
her transcendent charms, another more potent object. I
mean her immense profits, of which he longed to become a
sharer. There was no other way of gaining this point than
by professing himself her avowed admirer, which, we have
already seen, he did in a most effectual manner.

It has been already remarked that to the most engaging
person were added the most insinuating arts. We shall
not therefore enter into a further detail of his beauties, for
such they appeared in the eyes of every female beholder,
but proceed to the relation of matters of greater consequence.
Though they always lived in a state of the strictest unity
and love, yet their close connection, like that of matrimony,
how sweet soever it may be, was sometimes embittered
by little bickerings arising from the mutual jealousy

they entertained of each other ; thus it happened that the sweetness of their intimacy; which would otherwise have been very insipid, was tempered to such a degree by the acrimony of their differences, that their intimacy became the most agreeable imaginable.   It was like the acid, of which a proper quantity being infused in the composition of what is generally known by the name of punch, renders that liquor agreeable to the taste and grateful to the palate.

It cannot but be agreeable to our readers to mention a few of the trifling disputes which often happened between this loving pair; we shall therefore in order to gratify their wish, relate a few, though we must beg to be excused if, like Vellum in the comedy of *The Drummer, or the Haunted House*, we confine ourselves to three only.

The first which we find standing on record is one which occurred in consequence of her keeping a genteel footman, whom our officer considered as a rival to his happiness. The affair was as follows.   Our heroine was without a man-servant ; several were recommended to her, amongst whom was a young fellow of very genteel mien and address ; he was about eighteen, tall, handsome, and extremely well made.   He had not been many months in town, and was an utter stranger to the manners of it.   This simplicity gained him the approbation of Miss Catley, who never appeared so well pleased as when she was attended and served by him.   His obliging manner and the address with which he executed her commands, had made so great an impression on her, that she could no longer resist the temptation, and actually entertained a passion of the softest kind for him.   She was so unguarded as not to be able to help betraying it in her looks, and often, while he was waiting at table, could not help casting affectionate glances towards him.

This behaviour, though it was the effect of pure accident, was taken notice of by her lover; whose jealousy immediately taking fire, caused him to upbraid her in the strongest manner for her infidelity. This gave rise to a violent quarrel which lasted several days, during which time they did not see or speak to each other.

During this interval both parties were equally uneasy, and longed for a reconciliation, though neither made the smallest advance towards an accommodation.

Our heroine was the first to offer terms of peace. It was easily produced by the immediate discharge of the footman. Miss Catley however, out of regard, provided for him in a very decent manner till she could put him in another place, which she found an opportunity of doing in a very short time.

The next source of uneasiness which arose between this loving pair, was owing to the restless temper of Miss Catley, who having been one day to a noted milliner's in the Strand, to buy some rich laces, besides other goods furnished by those people, made use of in the article of dress, accidentally met her dear inamorata at the same place. Finding him in deep discourse with one of the young women behind the counter, she in her turn grew jealous, and was for a considerable time implacable in her resentment, which she took every opportunity of shewing. The lovers at length being heartily tired of living in this state of indifference, resolved to be reconciled, which was very easily brought to pass.

The third quarrel we shall mention owed its origin to the following accident. Miss C——y had once returned a very humorous answer to a *billet-doux* which was sent her one evening while she was performing at the theatre. Her lover was in the green room when she received it, and mistaking the contents of her answer, imagined she had given him an assignation. This occasioned a great altercation between them, which was succeeded by a mutual silence on each side, which lasted for above a month, although they saw each other and ate at the same table every day. Their reconciliation was brought about as follows. She, one day while they were at table, having eyed him attentively for some time, burst out into a loud fit of laughter, which he observing, put on a look which but too plainly showed the great displeasure he conceived at her behaviour. He still however maintained a profound silence, which she obliged him to break by extending her hands and speaking to him in these words : "My dear colonel, you are certainly very little versed in the ways of women, or you would be convinced that they are actuated principally by whim and caprice. You are therefore not to wonder at their actions, nor easily to take umbrage at what may at first sight appear a levity in their conduct. You were present when I received a note from the Earl of H——— and you saw me write an answer to it, which I should have shown you had I the least suspicion of your being jealous. To show you how little reason you have for this odd behaviour, I do assure you, and call heaven to witness, that I did not return any other answer to him than an order to admit one into the boxes, which plainly evinces how averse I was to any connection with him." He could contain no longer, but throwing his arms round about her neck, vowed eternal fidelity and love.

Thus did these two lovers re-assume their intercourse with greater ardour than before, and this peace, which indeed proved only temporary, lasted about six months.

Another unhappy accident occasioned a breach, which was as follows.

Her lover had for some time been confined to his bed by a violent fit of the gout, a disease he was very much subject to, and on his recovery had removed to country lodgings at Kensington, where our heroine visited him as often as she conveniently could find an opportunity. She went thither one day, having no employment at the theatre, to see him. She entered the apartment, but was surprised that she did not according to her expectation meet with him at home. She was not a little amazed to see several letters on his table, the superscriptions of which appeared to be written in a woman's hand. As they were opened her curiosity induced her to take up one, in which she read as follows :

" My dear,

I would have waited on you this evening, but was hindered by a female friend, who with irresistible force obliged me to accompany her to the play. I was on thorns during the whole time of the representation, and could not in consequence of the uneasiness which I suffered receive the least pleasure from what I was obliged to be present at. I hope, however, to-morrow to enjoy the pleasure of your agreeable company, to which, as you may be well convinced from the tenor of my whole behaviour hitherto, I shall fly, borne on the swiftest wings of love, to participate.

Yours eternally, N——."

This letter produced such an effect as is easy for the reader to guess. She left the house in a rage, vowed never to see him more, and every one of her actions shewed how much she took this seeming inconstancy of his to heart. She returned home in such agitation of spirits that she fell into fits almost instantaneously on entering her own house, and it was several days before she was entirely recovered. She could not by any means be prevailed on to repeat her visits to Kensington, to which place she did not once return during the whole time the Colonel remained there.   When he came to town she loaded him with the keenest reproaches, and was not reconciled to him for several weeks.   In vain did he assert his innocency, the letter she had seen was an incontestable proof of his guilt, and this quarrel must have necessarily terminated in a final separation, had not a friend of his, dining one day at the house of our heroine solved the riddle, by declaring it to be a letter he had received from his mistress and which he had sent to the Colonel for his perusal.   This declaration produced the desired effect, and a reconciliation presently took place.

Not to tire the reader with a repetition of these domestic feuds and uneasiness, we shall only mention one more, and then proceed to the relation of matters of greater importance. It happened in the following manner.   Our heroine having one evening appeared in the character of a virgin in a dramatic poem lately introduced on the stage, called *Elfrida*, had given so much pleasure and satisfaction to the Right Honourable Earl of D——, as great an admirer of, as he is a connoisseur in, the art of music, that his lordship could not help complimenting her, a few days after, with a ticket for the Pantheon.   She went thither in the habit of a shepherdess, and on this occasion had taken care not to omit anything that might be the least addition to her native beauty.   The Colonel accompanied her thither, dressed in a domino, and though a man of his polite breeding might be easily supposed to be thoroughly acquainted with such freedoms as the liberty of a place of that sort affords, yet

he could not forbear suffering his troublesome jealous spirit
to reign predominant in his breast on this occasion.
Observing that our heroine, imitating the other masks,
appeared more gay than ordinary, he was highly offended,
and took notice of it afterwards in terms which were highly
disagreeable to her. She resented this behaviour very
much, and refused to have anything to do with him for
several weeks, though he lodged at the same house with her.
At length, being unable to support this cessation of arms in
the cause of love, he acknowledged his error, asked her
pardon, and they became as cordial friends as before.

We may here relate an adventure which happened to our
heroine during the time of her connection with a young
wine merchant near Crutched Friars. He had seen her in
the piazza and had ordered his footman, who attended him,
to watch her home, and bring him word where she lived.
Having received the necessary information, he repaired the
next day to her lodgings and was well received by Miss
Catley, who was struck at the engaging appearance which
he made, and after about an hour's conversation they agreed
to see each other at an appointed place as often as
opportunity offered. Love, ever on the watch, soon
prompted one, and our heroine frequently made excursions
to White Conduit House, and they passed their leisure
hours in the most tender endearments. This lasted about
three years, during which period Miss Catley found
means to ingratiate herself into his good graces so far, that
at the end of it, she found herself about fifteen hundred
pounds in pocket, the fruits of this agreeable intrigue.
The adventure would have probably lasted much longer,
had she not been discovered by her inamorata when she
least expected it, in a private *tete-a-tete* with one of the

drawers belonging to a noted place of resort in the gardens. This caused a rupture between her and her gallant, and his animosity against her was so great that no persuasion could ever induce him to consent to a reconciliation with her.

The rest of our story is connected with an entirely new aspect of this singular woman's life, with the period dating from her marriage with the Colonel Lascelles. For several years she had lived with him merely as his mistress, during which time several children were born. Then her former levity gave way to domestic decorum, and her faults were only to be found in a retrospective view of her life. This behaviour raised such a disinterested and generous affection in the heart of her friend, that he resolved to bestow upon her the highest reward in his power, and actually made her his wife.

Nan would not be outdone in generosity; before she accepted the hand of the Colonel (for he was a Colonel when he married her) she insisted that certain preliminary articles should be ratified. The principal of these were, that her fortune should go to her children, that she should continue to play while her health permitted her, and that the marriage should be kept secret till she retired from the stage.

She did not however long continue in a public line, after she became a wife; the ensuing season she engaged with the manager of Covent Garden Theatre, and it proved the last of her appearances. Her voice was then considerably weakened, and her vivacity evidently diminished. She attempted the character of Macheath, in the *Beggars' Opera*, but she was then nothing better than the shadow and echo of what she had been, and her exertions to please only excited the pity, not the approbation, of the audience.

After leaving the stage she took up her abode at Ealing in Middlesex, and was much respected by the better sort of people in the neighbourhood, and beloved by the poor, to whom she became a beneficent friend. She died in this retirement, in the 44th year of her age, and was buried in Ealing Church, with every mark of attention and respect that a husband could possibly shew to a wife whom he tenderly loved.

Her disease was a consumption, to which she had been inclined from her youth, and which probably was accelerated by her early indulgencies in dissipation, and great exertion of voice which injured her lungs. She bore its progress with resignation, and died in that most enviable of all states, at peace with the world, and in strong hopes of eternal bliss.

Miss Catley had great capabilities for an actress, and notwithstanding her vivacious appearance would have succeeded not only in comedy, but tragedy, had she made them her study ; but her voice was so exquisite, she had no occasion for further aid. Its native strains exceeded the vocal powers of all who went before her, yet she often evinced a deficiency of judgment.

Rosetta in *Love in a Village*, and Euphrosyne in *Comus*, were her best performances. In the latter it may not be going too far to assert she never was equalled, particularly in the song of "The wanton god that pierces hearts," which she gave in a characteristic style of levity, that left all competition at a distance. And in the former, her singing was truly exquisite and replete with native humour. Soon after the affair with Lord R—— and the roast duck, which has been stated, that nobleman came into the stage-box whilst she was singing "The wanton god," and when she came to the line "No squeamish fop shall spoil my rest," she turned full upon his lordship with a look of archness, so pointed and so marked with contempt, that the mortified nobleman rose from his seat and left her to enjoy the thundering plaudits of the audience, which were given in peals accompanied by bursts of laughter.

In *The Maid of the Mill* she often performed Patty, and not without pathos, and when Mrs. Abingdon was in Ireland, during the late Mr. Mossop's management, Catley often performed in a style of the highest spirit and humour Captain Flash, in contrast to the other lady's Fribble, which was also excellent. Catley was not vain, for though she took every possible pains to set off her person and face to advantage when she appeared in juvenile parts, yet, as the representative of old Dorcas in *Thomas and Sally*, she was equally attentive to appear ancient.

Catley was not beautiful but pleasing. Her face was oval, her features *petite*, and her eyes small; her forehead being remarkably high, she always wore her dark hair, which was thin and lank, cut down upon it like a fan, and this at last became a general fashion under the denomination of Catlified hair, and as it gives a peculiar archness to the countenance, remained in vogue for years among the lower classes of those ladies who stroll the streets.

Catley was remarkably thin, her bones small, her skin brown, and all covered over with freckles, yet her *tout ensemble* was pleasing, when she was made up and on the stage.

Much has been said of Miss Catley's wit, by those who have mistaken her talent; her *bon mots* were those of broad and vulgar humour, they were deficient in that polish sharpness and neatness, which produce the genuine brightness of conversation, her points were not those of raillery, but of railing, they came out gross, as if issuing from a cellar in St. Giles's, or, which was the fact, as if they had received their original impression in a garret near the Tower.

A retrospect of Miss Catley's life when compared with that of the celebrated Nell Gwynn, exhibits many incidents of strong similitude. Nell was born of obscure parents, so was Nan. Nell was born in a cellar in the Coal-yard, Drury-lane; Nan was born in a garret in a wretched alley near Tower-hill. Nell, when first taken notice of, sold oranges, and resorted to public houses. Nan, when young, sang in alehouses for hire. Nell when almost a child was decoyed from the path of virtue by a merchant; Nan suffered similarly soon after entering her teens, at the hands of a linen draper. Nell was remarkable for smartness of conversation, so was Nan. Nell was an actress in great vogue, so was Nan. To Nell, lords and dukes paid their addresses, so they did to Nan. Nell was the mistress of a king, Nan that of a prince of the blood royal.

> " This shews that sultans, emperors, and kings,
>   When blood boils high will stoop to meanest things."

Nell was of a gay frolicksome disposition, so was Nan; of Nell many droll passages have been reported, so of Nan, but in respect to both ladies, some of their sayings should be suppressed as being too loose for the public ear.

Nell's air was free and *degagée*, so was the carriage of Nan. Nell had spirit and pleasantry, so had Nan. She had professed more charity and generosity than most women of her situation in life, so did Nan, and here an instance may be given, which illustrates this part of our

heroine's character.   Mr. Linton, a musician belonging to
Covent Garden Theatre, having been inhumanly murdered
by footpads, Mr. Harris the manager, gave his widow and
children a free benefit.   A short time previous to the
benefit night, Nan went to a masquerade in the character
of an orange girl, with several dozen box tickets in her
basket, these she disposed of among the company for a very
considerable sum over their usual price, which with ten
guineas added by herself, she sent the next day to the
unfortunate family.

As in their lives, so in their deaths, there was a strong
similarity between Nell Gwynne and Ann Catley, except
that Nell lived to be much older than Nan.   But she
certainly died with a moral and religious mind, or Dr.
Tenison, afterwards Archbishop of Canterbury, would not
have preached her funeral sermon.   And this was the
opinion of Queen Mary, who, when the Earl of Jersey
urged the circumstance to prevent the doctor's preferment
to the diocese of Lincoln, answered, " It was a sign that
this unfortunate woman died penitent, for if I can read a
man's heart through his looks, had she not made a truly
pious and christian end, the doctor would never have been
induced to speak well of her."   Just such an end did Catley
make, dying in charity with the world, and in lamenting
that the early parts of her life had not been equally
virtuous and honourable with her latter days.

A writer in the *History of the English Stage* says,
" Her goodness of heart and benignity of disposition
appear in many charitable works which would have done
honour to more high-born dames ; her wanderings cannot
be called errors, but *misfortunes*, the common result of
a bad education.   Though she came into the world without

E

reputation, she left it with a *good character*, a sufficient proof that all her levities proceeded from inexperience and not from natural depravity."

The following eulogium was paid to her memory in the public prints :

"She was the favourite of Thalia, the favourite of the Town, and the favourite of Fortune.

Her theatrical representations will be remembered as long as the fame exists of the poets that pourtrayed them. The discussion of her professional merit should be the subject of a volume ; we shall therefore only add, that her voice and manner were, perhaps, never equalled in the same style. Her person *all but* equalled her accomplishments, and nearly to her death she was the centre of attraction.

Beauty is a captivating syren, and to resist her enchantments man must possess something *more* or something *less* than the usual portion of humanity. The allurements a theatrical life holds out to lovely women, admit the same observation, and justify the application with tenfold force. All that can be said is, Alas poor human nature ! She possessed many virtues, and the greatest of all— humanity. The generous hand often *lightened* the *heavy* heart. Feelingly alive by nature to every impression of sensibility, this amiable virtue accompanied her elevation to rank and riches, and joined others that adorn the first stations in society, and which alone make them respectable. She was the good mother, the chaste wife and accomplished woman. Prudery certainly formed no part of her character, but where is the prude that ever owned half her merit ! Her openness, goodness, knowledge and generosity, added to her personal accomplishments, rendered her an acquisition of which the worthiest might be proud. This morality of players, like that of princes, is exempt from the precision of vulgar rules."

INSCRIPTION

Engraved on a tree at George Stainforth, Esq's., in Hertford-shire, formerly the cottage of Anne Catley.

> Catley, the once famed Syren of the stage,
> Melodious heroine of a former age,
> Her labours o'er, here fix'd her glad retreat ;
> These her lov'd fields, and this her fav'rite seat.
> Hither at early dawn she bent her way,
> To mark the progress of the new mown hay ;
> Partook the toil, joined gaily in the throng,
> And often cheer'd the rustics with a song ;
> Nor with a song alone, her liberal heart
> In all their little sorrows bore a part,
> And as they simply told their tale of grief,
> Her head gave counsel and her hand relief.
> Let not the *wedded* dame who wanders here,
> Disdain o'er Catley's turf to shed a tear ;
> Nor the fond virgin, sheltered by this tree,
> Withhold the drop of sensibility.
> What though stern Hymen may no sanction give
> In nature's tenderest page the tear shall live ;
> An anxious parent, to her offspring just,
> True to her promise, sacred to her trust ;
> Firm in her friendship, faithful in her love,—
> Who will the mourn'd remembrance disapprove ?

THE celebrated Anne Catley, formerly a member of Covent Garden Theatre, died the beginning of this season (Oct. 14, 1789), at General Lascelles' house, near Brentford, to whom it is said she was married.

This lady was a striking example of what merit can do, unaided by birth or interest. She was born in 1745, in an

Alley, near Tower Hill,—" of parentage obscure,"—her
father being a hackney coachman (afterwards the keeper of
a public house near Norwood), and her mother a washerwoman. Her extraordinary vocal abilities soon discovered
themselves, for at the early age of ten years she sung at
public houses in her father's neighbourhood, and for the
officers on duty at the tower ; her situation of course exposed
her to seduction—but who that considers her then helpless
condition of life, will not curse the *seducer*, and pity the
seduced !

Her musical talents soon spread their own fame ; and one
Bates, a musician, who lived in the west end of the town,
entered into an article with her father and took her
apprentice ; but Bates and Catley could not agree, and the
former, it is said, was once so provoked as to threaten to
turn her out of doors, and sue her father for £200, the
penalty of the bond executed when she was bound.

Her first appearance was at Vauxhall, in the summer of
1762, and on the 8th of October in the same year she
appeared for the first time on the stage at Covent Garden,
in the character of the Pastoral Nymph, in *Comus.*

The succeeding year she became the object of public
attention from a very remarkable circumstance : Sir Francis
Blake Delaval, being smitten with her beauty, and understanding that the master and fair apprentice could not
agree, resolved on releasing her entirely from the coercion
of Mr. Bates, and making her his mistress. Accordingly it
was agreed that Sir Francis should pay Bates the penalty
of the father's bond, and also give him two hundred pounds
more in lieu of what she might earn for him, by the engagement he had made for her with the managers of Covent
Garden Theatre and Marybone Gardens. For this purpose

Mr. Fraine, an attorney, was ordered to draw up a proper transfer of her indentures from Bates to Sir Francis ; and she and her mother were removed into lodgings, where she lived publicly with Sir Francis, was attended by his servants, and rode out with him every day.

The attorney having made the father a party to the articles, waited on him to have his signature and seal. Mr. Catley lived at this time with the very respectable Mr. Barclay, of Cheapside, as private coachman, and having got possession of the articles, consulted his master on the nature of them. The honest quaker, shocked at the wickedness of transferring a girl, by legal process, for the purpose of prostitution, advised with his lawyer, who laid a case before counsel, and the ensuing term two motions were made to the court founded on these articles.

The first of these motions was for a *habeas corpus*, directed to Sir Francis Blake Delaval, to bring the body of Anne Catley into court. The second was for a rule to shew cause why an information should not be granted against Sir Francis Blake Delaval, Bates the master, and Fraine the attorney, for a conspiracy to prostitute Anne Catley, under the forms of law.

On the ensuing day, our heroine, in consequence of the *habeas corpus*, appeared in court, accompanied by Sir Francis, and was then discharged out of his custody ; the affidavits for the prosecutor were read, and a day was fixed for cause to be shewn. On the lady's release, her father attempted to seize her and carry her off by force. Sir Fletcher Norton, counsel for Sir Francis, immediately complained to the court, and the violent conduct of the father was very severely reprimanded by the Chief Justice, Earl Mansfield, who observed that, though the girl was not of legal age, she was at full years of discretion; and the question being put, whether she would return with her father or Sir Francis, she declared her attachment to the latter, put her hand under his arm, and making a curtsey to the Judges, and another to the bar, walked with him out of Westminster Hall, to his carriage, which waited at the gate, and carried them home.

On cause being shown, the court was clearly of opinion that the information should be granted. Lord Mansfield observed that the court of King's Bench was *custos morum* of the country, and had authority, especially where the offence was mixed with conspiracy, to punish everything *contra bonos mores.* He called the premium given by Sir Francis to Bates *premium prostitutionis*, and cited the case of Sir Richard Sedley in the reign of Charles II. to prove it.

The consequence of this information against Sir Francis, Bates, and Fraine, was a trial, and all the defendants being found guilty by the jury, were severally fined, the whole expense of which (with the costs to a very considerable amount) fell npon Sir Francis.

After this she sung at Marybone Gardens, and became a pupil of Mr. Macklin, who procured her an engagement at Dublin from Mossop, where she met with great success and brought crowded houses. Many anecdotes are related of her while on her visit to Dublin; the following are the most remarkable. A merchant, with a wife and family, having been smitten by her charms, sent her a *billet-doux* requesting an appointment to supper, and accompanied his request with a large hamper of champagne. Catley returned the wine untouched, with a direction to the amorous trader's spouse, enclosing his note under a cover. At supper the wife declared she had a longing for champagne, and must have a glass; the husband reprobated such extravagance. "But I will treat you, my dear," said the wife, "you may see I have received a present," on which she put Catley's note into his hands. It is easy to conceive the domestic quarrel that ensued, and the person here alluded to has for years back lived in London in the most indigent circumstances.

When Dean Bailey was a principal superintendent to the public charities of Dublin, it was determined by the governors that a concert should be performed for the benefit of the Lying-in-Hospital, whereupon the Dean took it upon him to engage Catley as a singer, and wrote her a card requesting that she would give him a *night*, and mention when she should be *disengaged*. The answer was that Miss Catley was specially engaged for a week, but after that time, as the Dean was a charitable man, she would give him a *night gratis*. Our heroine kept her word, to the great emolument of the hospital, and told the story, which produced a general laugh against the ecclesiastic.

She paid another visit to Dublin during Ryder's management, when her Juno, in the *Golden Pippin*, was highly applauded, and her song of "Push about the Jorum" universally encored. Perhaps the manner of performing burlettas there, where the recitative is generally spoken as dialogue, afforded her a greater opportunity of displaying that peculiar vivacity which scorned all bounds, except those of decorum.

In 1770 she appeared again at Covent Garden, and continued to perform a stated number of nights for many succeeding years, much to her own and the manager's advantage. In 1773, she sung at the oratorios at Covent Garden, by which she added to her fortune more than her fame, for her natural vivacity was not well suited to the solemnity of such performances, and had to contend with the more chastised deportment of Mr. Sheridan at the rival theatre. Being always attentive to economy, in a course of years she had amassed a considerable fortune, and when her attractions failed, she was enabled to retire to independence. Her last performance was in 1784.

Her goodness of heart and benignity of disposition appear in many charitable works, which would have done honour to more high-born dames ; her wanderings cannot be called errors, but misfortunes, the common result of a bad education.   Though she came into the world without reputation, she left it with a good character, a sufficient proof that all her levities proceeded from inexperience, and not from natural depravity.

Though she was no wit, she possessed a considerable share of humour, several *bon mots*, however, have been made for her, such as she would be ashamed to utter, for good nature and decency were inseparable companions of her mirth.   To the man of her choice she was faithful, loving, and submissive, though on the stage the best Juno that ever boxed a Jupiter.

Characters Performed by Miss Catley.

1763.—COVENT GARDEN.
April 26th   "Sally," in *Love makes a Man.*

1763.—DUBLIN.
Mossop invited her to Dublin; she arrived in December,
and made her first appearance as "Polly Peachum."

1764.—SMOCK ALLEY, DUBLIN.
October 15th   "Polly" and "Macheath."
"Patty," in the *Maid of the Mill.*

1765.—SMOCK ALLEY, DUBLIN.
As "Polly" and "Lucy."

1769.—SMOCK ALLEY, DUBLIN.
March   As "Euphrosyne," in *Comus.*
Oct. 11th   As "Polly," also "Euphrosyne."

1770.—COVENT GARDEN.
October 2nd   As "Rosetta," in *Love in a Village.*
„   23rd   As "Leonora," in *Venice Preserved.*
Novem. 8th   As "Jenny," in *Lionel and Clarissa.*
„   22nd   As "Isabella," in *The Portrait.*
(Never before acted.)
Decem. 13th   As "Rachel," in the *Jovial Crew.*

1772.—SMOCK ALLEY, DUBLIN.
As "Rosetta," several times.   As "Polly" once.
As "Euphrosyne" once, when she took a benefit.

1772.—COVENT GARDEN.
Sept. 30th   First appearance for two years in "Rosetta."
Oct. 13th   As "Polly," in the *Beggars' Opera.*
„   17th   In Chorus of British Virgins, in *Elfrida.*
(Never before acted.)

1773.—COVENT GARDEN.

February 6th   As " Juno," in the *Golden Pippin.*

Septem. 16th   As " Euphrosyne," in *Comus ;* also in the
West Indian.

Decem. 16th   As " Theaspe," in *Achilles in Petticoats ;*
also as " Earl of Essex."

1774.—COVENT GARDEN.

Septem.   5th   As " Lucy " (1st time), in *Beggars' Opera.*

Novem.   1st   As " Rachel," in the *Jovial Crew.*

1775.—COVENT GARDEN.

January 21st   As " Harriet," in the *Two Misers ;* also in
Henry II.

1776.—COVENT GARDEN.

Septem. 27th   As " Polly," in the *Beggars' Opera.*

„   30th   As " Lucy,"   do.

October 25th   As " Rachel," in the *Jovial Crew.*

1780.—COVENT GARDEN.

Feby.   17th   As " Euphrosyne," in *Comus.*

Septem. 20th   As " Clara" (1st time), in *The Duenna.*

„   21st   As " Lucy," in the *Beggars' Opera.*

Novem. 15th   As " Aunt Deborah " (by desire, and with a
Song in character).

Decem. 12th   As " Dorcas," in the *Spanish Friar.*
(By desire.)

1781.—COVENT GARDEN.

January 13th   As " Fanny," in the *Maid of the Mill.*

October 17th   As " Macheath," in the *Beggars' Opera.*

1782.—COVENT GARDEN.

March   18th   As " Margery," in the *Mourning Bride*
(for Miss Younge's benefit.)

Miss Catley as Macbeath.

To the Printer of the Town and Country Magazine.

Sir,

The different Metamorphoses which the *Beggars' Opera* has lately undergone, clearly prove that burlesque and ridicule may be carried too far. It is more than probable that Mr. Colman took his idea of transposing the characters from males to females, and *vice versa*, from the success Mrs. Kennedy had met with in "Macheath;" the thought, however, appeared novel, and it succeeded beyond his most sanguine expectations. The managers of Covent Garden Theatre, unwilling to be outdone in invention, judged, that in representing all the characters by females they would improve upon Mr. Colman's thought, and Miss Catley was chosen, at a very extravagant salary, to perform *Macheath ;* but her greatest admirers must own, that she neither looked, dressed, or spoke the character, so as to convey the idea of a bold, enterprising gentleman highwayman. For what cause is best known to herself, she never changed her dress, but appeared in boots the whole time, as if she were just come off the road ; whereas *Macheath* always dressed previous to his going to Marybone, as it is to be supposed he was there to meet some of the politest company about town, to whom he would take every precaution of not giving the slightest suspicion of his being a highwayman. The consequence was natural, and, as might be expected, the town was nauseated with the same unnatural hodge-podge, though dressed different ways, and they repaired to another table that was better served.

In a word Miss Catley has been fairly foiled at her own weapons. She judged that by brazening out the part she was sure of success; whilst Mrs. Cargill, by studying nature, and pursuing the intention of the poet, not only succeeded in the same character beyond her friends' most sanguine expectations, but, it is said, that she looked so much "the youth in a cart who has the air of a lord," that she made some conquests amongst her own sex, who were unapprized of the deception.   THEATRICUS.

O'Keeffe and Miss Catley.

O'KEEFFE says "The first time of my venturing into a theatre after the ill success of my '*Banditti*,' Miss Catley accosted me from a front now of the lower boxes, loud enough, as I was many rows back, to be heard by all and everybody, ' So, O'Keeffe you had a piece damned the other night—I'm glad of it—the devil mend you for writing an Opera without bringing me into it. '

A few minutes after she had thus accosted me, Leoni entered the box, with a lady leaning on his arm—Miss Catley catching his eye, called out, 'How do you do Leoni ? I hear you're married—is that your wife ! bid her stand up till I see her.' Leoni, abashed, whispered the lady, who, with good humoured compliance stood up—Catley after surveying her a little, said, ' Ha ! very well indeed—I like your choice.' The audience around seemed more diverted with this scene in the boxes than that on the stage, as Miss Catley and her oddities were well known to all."

Death of Miss Catley.

THE family of Catley coming from Yorkshire, I am
reminded of the decease of a favourite of that name, the
celebrated Anne Catley, whom I could only know, when
a visible decline was sapping the vital power that bore
her once triumphantly above all humorous singers.

Miss Catley, was, I think, married to General Lascelles,
and left a large family by him, four sons and four
daughters—however her will was signed Anne Catley, and
was written entirely in her own hand.   The good sense
that she unquestionably possessed, appears eminently in
the final settlement of her property.   She makes General
Francis Lascelles sole executor, and bequeaths him ten
pounds for a mourning ring.   The eldest of her four
daughters at the time of her decease, was to have her
wearing apparel, watch, trinkets, &c., as a distinction—
in all other respects, the four sons and four daughters
were to have equal shares at the age of twenty-one years ;
and, until then, their shares were to be invested in the
funds, and considered, as to the interest, applicable to
their education.   She had bought the house in which she
died, at Ealing for the daughters, and, as far as a provident
parent could do, established them respectably.   The
probate called her property £5000, but this was far from
being the whole of it.

There was in her personal character a good deal of the
careless boldness of Woffington ; like her too she was
extremely handsome, and her eye and mouth had a peculiar
expression of archness.   She aimed at an almost manly
frankness of speech, and acted as one superior to censure

when she raised the wonder of prudery. Catley had an understanding too sound to indicate the indiscretions of her youth ; but her follies did not long survive that period, and she amply atoned in her maturity for the scandal she had excited formerly in society. There was a graceful propriety in her domestic concerns. She was never profuse, and could therefore be liberal in all her arrangements. In her youth she had been acquainted with difficulties, and the lesson was ever present to her mind. Her ear was always open to the unhappy, and her hand was enabled, by economy, to spare no scanty relief to strangers, without invading the provision she had destined for her family. In the great relations of life as a daughter, wife, mother, and friend, she was, in principle, steady and exemplary.

Her complaint, a pulmonary consumption, had wasted her to a shade, and it had lingered beyond the usual term of that baneful, yet flattering pest. She was but forty-four at the time of her decease. There were many points of similarity between Mrs. Jordan and Miss Catley ; not that the former ever possessed the *nerve* or the *prudence* of the latter.—*Life of Mrs. Jordan*, BOADEN.

FINIS.

Music and Books published by Travis & Emery Music Bookshop:

Anon.: Hymnarium Sarisburiense, cum Rubricis et Notis Musicis.

Agricola, Johann Friedrich from Tosi: Anleitung zur Singkunst.

Bach, C.P.E.: edited W. Emery: Nekrolog or Obituary Notice of J.S. Bach.

Bateson, Naomi Judith: Alcock of Salisbury

Bathe, William: A Briefe Introduction to the Skill of Song

Bax, Arnold: Symphony #5, Arranged for Piano Four Hands by Walter Emery

Burney, Charles: The Present State of Music in France and Italy

Burney, Charles: The Present State of Music in Germany, The Netherlands ...

Burney, Charles: An Account of the Musical Performances ... Handel

Burney, Karl: Nachricht von Georg Friedrich Handel's Lebensumstanden.

Burns, Robert: The Caledonian Musical Museum ..The Best Scotch Songs. (1810)

Cobbett, W.W.: Cobbett's Cyclopedic Survey of Chamber Music. (2 vols.)

Corrette, Michel: Le Maitre de Clavecin

Crimp, Bryan: Dear Mr. Rosenthal ... Dear Mr. Gaisberg ...

Crimp, Bryan: Solo: The Biography of Solomon

d'Indy, Vincent: Beethoven: Biographie Critique

d'Indy, Vincent: Beethoven: A Critical Biography

d'Indy, Vincent: César Franck (in French)

Fischhof, Joseph: Versuch einer Geschichte des Clavierbaues. (Faksimile 1853).

Frescobaldi, Girolamo: D'Arie Musicali per Cantarsi. Primo & Secondo Libro.

Geminiani, Francesco: The Art of Playing the Violin.

Handel; Purcell; Boyce; Geene et al: Calliope or English Harmony: Volume First.

Häuser: Musikalisches Lexikon. 2 vols in one.

Hawkins, John: A General History of the Science and Practice of Music (5 vols.)

Herbert-Caesari, Edgar: The Science and Sensations of Vocal Tone

Herbert-Caesari, Edgar: Vocal Truth

Hopkins and Rimboult: The Organ. Its History and Construction.

Hunt, John: - see separate list of discographies at the end of these titles

Isaacs, Lewis: Hänsel and Gretel. A Guide to Humperdinck's Opera.

Isaacs, Lewis: Königskinder (Royal Children) A Guide to Humperdinck's Opera.

Kastner: Manuel Général de Musique Militaire

Lacassagne, M. l'Abbé Joseph : Traité Général des élémens du Chant.

Lascelles (née Catley), Anne: The Life of Miss Anne Catley.

Mainwaring, John: Memoirs of the Life of the Late George Frederic Handel

Malcolm, Alexander: A Treaty of Music: Speculative, Practical and Historical

Marx, Adolph Bernhard: Die Kunst des Gesanges, Theoretisch-Practisch

May, Florence: The Life of Brahms

May, Florence: The Girlhood Of Clara Schumann: Clara Wieck And Her Time.

Mellers, Wilfrid: Angels of the Night: Popular Female Singers of Our Time

Mellers, Wilfrid: Bach and the Dance of God

Mellers, Wilfrid: Beethoven and the Voice of God

Mellers, Wilfrid: Caliban Reborn - Renewal in Twentieth Century Music

Music and Books published by Travis & Emery Music Bookshop:

Mellers, Wilfrid: Darker Shade of Pale, A Backdrop to Bob Dylan
Mellers, Wilfrid: François Couperin and the French Classical Tradition
Mellers, Wilfrid: Harmonious Meeting
Mellers, Wilfrid: Le Jardin Retrouvé, The Music of Frederic Mompou
Mellers, Wilfrid: Music and Society, England and the European Tradition
Mellers, Wilfrid: Music in a New Found Land: ... ... American Music
Mellers, Wilfrid: Romanticism and the Twentieth Century (from 1800)
Mellers, Wilfrid: The Masks of Orpheus: ...... the Story of European Music.
Mellers, Wilfrid: The Sonata Principle (from c. 1750)
Mellers, Wilfrid: Vaughan Williams and the Vision of Albion
Panchianio, Cattuffio: Rutzvanscad Il Giovine
Pearce, Charles: Sims Reeves, Fifty Years of Music in England.
Playford, John: An Introduction to the Skill of Musick.
Purcell, Henry et al: Harmonia Sacra ... The First Book, (1726)
Purcell, Henry et al: Harmonia Sacra ... Book II (1726)
Quantz, Johann: Versuch einer Anweisung die Flöte trave rsiere zu spielen.
Rameau, Jean-Philippe: Code de Musique Pratique, ou Methodes.
Rastall, Richard: The Notation of Western Music.
Rimbault, Edward: The Pianoforte, Its Origins, Progress, and Construction.
Rousseau, Jean Jacques: Dictionnaire de Musique
Rubinstein, Anton : Guide to the proper use of the Pianoforte Pedals.
Sainsbury, John S.: Dictionary of Musicians. (1825). 2 vols.
Serré de Rieux, Jean de : Les dons des Enfans de Latone
Simpson, Christopher: A Compendium of Practical Musick in Five Parts
Spohr, Louis: Autobiography
Spohr, Louis: Grand Violin School
Tans'ur, William: A New Musical Grammar; or The Harmonical Spectator
Terry, Charles Sanford: Bach's Chorals – Parts 1, 2 and 3.
Terry, Charles Sanford: John Christian Bach
Terry, Charles Sanford: J.S. Bach's Original Hymn-Tunes for Congregational Use.
Terry, Charles Sanford: Four-Part Chorals of J.S. Bach. (German & English)
Terry, Charles Sanford: Joh. Seb. Bach, Cantata Texts, Sacred and Secular.
Terry, Charles Sanford: The Origins of the Family of Bach Musicians.
Tosi, Pierfrancesco: Opinioni de' Cantori Antichi, e Moderni
Tosi, Pierfrancesco: Observations on the Florid Song.
Van der Straeten, Edmund: History of the Violoncello, The Viol da Gamba ...
Van der Straeten, Edmund: History of the Violin, Its Ancestors... (2 vols.)
Walther, J. G. [Waltern]: Musicalisches Lexikon [Musikalisches Lexicon]
Zwirn, Gerald: Stranded Stories From The Operas

Travis & Emery Music Bookshop
17 Cecil Court, London, WC2N 4EZ, United Kingdom.
Tel. (+44) 20 7240 2129

© Travis & Emery 2010

Discographies by Travis & Emery:
Discographies by John Hunt.

1987: 978-1-906857-14-1: From Adam to Webern: the Recordings of von Karajan.

1991: 978-0-951026-83-0: 3 Italian Conductors and 7 Viennese Sopranos: 10 Discographies: Arturo Toscanini, Guido Cantelli, Carlo Maria Giulini, Elisabeth Schwarzkopf, Irmgard Seefried, Elisabeth Gruemmer, Sena Jurinac, Hilde Gueden, Lisa Della Casa, Rita Streich.

1992: 978-0-951026-85-4: Mid-Century Conductors and More Viennese Singers: 10 Discographies: Karl Boehm, Victor De Sabata, Hans Knappertsbusch, Tullio Serafin, Clemens Krauss, Anton Dermota, Leonie Rysanek, Eberhard Waechter, Maria Reining, Erich Kunz.

1993: 978-0-951026-87-8: More 20th Century Conductors: 7 Discographies: Eugen Jochum, Ferenc Fricsay, Carl Schuricht, Felix Weingartner, Josef Krips, Otto Klemperer, Erich Kleiber.

1994: 978-0-951026-88-5: Giants of the Keyboard: 6 Discographies: Wilhelm Kempff, Walter Gieseking, Edwin Fischer, Clara Haskil, Wilhelm Backhaus, Artur Schnabel.

1994: 978-0-951026-89-2: Six Wagnerian Sopranos: 6 Discographies: Frieda Leider, Kirsten Flagstad, Astrid Varnay, Martha Moedl, Birgit Nilsson, Gwyneth Jones.

1995: 978-0-952582-70-0: Musical Knights: 6 Discographies: Henry Wood, Thomas Beecham, Adrian Boult, John Barbirolli, Reginald Goodall, Malcolm Sargent.

1995: 978-0-952582-71-7: A Notable Quartet: 4 Discographies: Gundula Janowitz, Christa Ludwig, Nicolai Gedda, Dietrich Fischer-Dieskau.

1996: 978-0-952582-75-5: Leopold Stokowski (1882-1977): Discography and Concert Register

1996: 978-0-952582-76-2: Makers of the Philharmonia: 11 Discographies: Alceo Galliera, Walter Susskind, Paul Kletzki, Nicolai Malko, Issay Dobrowen, Lovro Von Matacic, Efrem Kurtz, Otto Ackermann, Anatole Fistoulari, George Weldon, Robert Irving.

1996: 978-0-952582-72-4: The Post-War German Tradition: 5 Discographies: Rudolf Kempe, Joseph Keilberth, Wolfgang Sawallisch, Rafael Kubelik, Andre Cluytens.

1996: 978-0-952582-73-1: Teachers and Pupils: 7 Discographies: Elisabeth Schwarzkopf, Maria Ivoguen, Maria Cebotari, Meta Seinemeyer, Ljuba Welitsch, Rita Streich, Erna Berger.

1996: 978-0-952582-75-5: Leopold Stokowski: Discography and Concert Listing.

1996: 978-0-952582-76-2: Makers of the Philharmonia: 11 Discographies Alceo Galliera, Walter Susskind, Paul Kletzki, Nicolai Malko, Issay Dobrowen, Lovro Von Matacic, Efrem Kurtz, Otto Ackermann, Anatole Fistoulari, George Weldon, Robert Irving.

1996: 978-0-952582-77-9: Tenors in a Lyric Tradition: 3 Discographies: Peter Anders, Walther Ludwig, Fritz Wunderlich.

1997: 978-0-952582-78-6: The Lyric Baritone: 5 Discographies: Hans Reinmar, Gerhard Huesch, Josef Metternich, Hermann Uhde, Eberhard Waechter.

1997: 978-0-952582-79-3: Hungarians in Exile: 3 Discographies: Fritz Reiner, Antal Dorati, George Szell.

1997: 978-1-901395-00-6: The Art of the Diva: 3 Discographies: Claudia Muzio, Maria Callas, Magda Olivero.

1997: 978-1-901395-01-3: Metropolitan Sopranos: 4 Discographies: Rosa Ponselle, Eleanor Steber, Zinka Milanov, Leontyne Price.

1997: 978-1-901395-02-0: Back From The Shadows: 4 Discographies: Willem Mengelberg, Dimitri Mitropoulos, Hermann Abendroth, Eduard Van Beinum.

1997: 978-1-901395-03-7: More Musical Knights: 4 Discographies: Hamilton Harty, Charles Mackerras, Simon Rattle, John Pritchard.

1998: 978-1-901395-95-2: More Giants of the Keyboard: 5 Discographies: Claudio Arrau, Gyorgy Cziffra, Vladimir Horowitz, Dinu Lipatti, Artur Rubinstein.

1998: 978-1-901395-94-5: Conductors On The Yellow Label: 8 Discographies: Fritz Lehmann, Ferdinand Leitner, Ferenc Fricsay, Eugen Jochum, Leopold Ludwig, Artur Rother, Franz Konwitschny, Igor Markevitch.

1998: 978-1-901395-96-9: Mezzo and Contraltos: 5 Discographies: Janet Baker, Margarete Klose, Kathleen Ferrier, Giulietta Simionato, Elisabeth Hoengen.

1999: 978-1-901395-97-6: The Furtwaengler Sound Sixth Edition: Discography and Concert Listing.

1999: 978-1-901395-98-3: The Great Dictators: 3 Discographies: Evgeny Mravinsky, Artur Rodzinski, Sergiu Celibidache.

1999: 978-1-901395-99-0: Sviatoslav Richter: Pianist of the Century: Discography.

2000: 978-1-901395-04-4: Philharmonic Autocrat 1: Discography of: Herbert Von Karajan [Third Edition].

2000: 978-1-901395-05-1: Wiener Philharmoniker 1 - Vienna Philharmonic and Vienna State Opera Orchestras: Discography Part 1 1905-1954.

2000: 978-1-901395-06-8: Wiener Philharmoniker 2 - Vienna Philharmonic and Vienna State Opera Orchestras: Discography Part 2 1954-1989.

2001: 978-1-901395-07-5: Gramophone Stalwarts: 3 Separate Discographies: Bruno Walter, Erich Leinsdorf, Georg Solti.

2001: 978-1-901395-08-2: Singers of the Third Reich: 5 Discographies: Helge Roswaenge, Tiana Lemnitz, Franz Voelker, Maria Mueller, Max Lorenz.

2001: 978-1-901395-09-9: Philharmonic Autocrat 2: Concert Register of Herbert Von Karajan Second Edition.

2002: 978-1-901395-10-5: Sächsische Staatskapelle Dresden: Complete Discography.

2002: 978-1-901395-11-2: Carlo Maria Giulini: Discography and Concert Register.

2002: 978-1-901395-12-9: Pianists For The Connoisseur: 6 Discographies: Arturo Benedetti Michelangeli, Alfred Cortot, Alexis Weissenberg, Clifford Curzon, Solomon, Elly Ney.

2003: 978-1-901395-14-3: Singers on the Yellow Label: 7 Discographies: Maria Stader, Elfriede Troetschel, Annelies Kupper, Wolfgang Windgassen, Ernst Haefliger, Josef Greindl, Kim Borg.

2003: 978-1-901395-15-0: A Gallic Trio: 3 Discographies: Charles Muench, Paul Paray, Pierre Monteux.

2004: 978-1-901395-16-7: Antal Dorati 1906-1988: Discography and Concert Register.

2004: 978-1-901395-17-4: Columbia 33CX Label Discography.

2004: 978-1-901395-18-1: Great Violinists: 3 Discographies: David Oistrakh, Wolfgang Schneiderhan, Arthur Grumiaux.

2006: 978-1-901395-19-8: Leopold Stokowski: Second Edition of the Discography.

2006: 978-1-901395-20-4: Wagner Im Festspielhaus: Discography of the Bayreuth Festival.

2006: 978-1-901395-21-1: Her Master's Voice: Concert Register and Discography of Dame Elisabeth Schwarzkopf [Third Edition].

2007: 978-1-901395-22-8: Hans Knappertsbusch: Kna: Concert Register and Discography of Hans Knappertsbusch, 1888-1965. Second Edition.

2008: 978-1-901395-23-5: Philips Minigroove: Second Extended Version of the European Discography.

2009: 978-1-901395-24-2: American Classics: The Discographies of Leonard Bernstein and Eugene Ormandy.

2010: 978-1-901395-25-9: Dirigenten der DDR: Conductors of the German Democratic Republic

Discography by Stephen J. Pettitt, edited by John Hunt:

1987: 978-1-906857-16-5: Philharmonia Orchestra: Complete Discography 1945-1987

Available from: Travis & Emery at 17 Cecil Court, London, UK. (+44) 20 7 240 2129. email on sales@travis-and-emery.com .

www.ingramcontent.com/pod-product-compliance
Lightning Source LLC
Chambersburg PA
CBHW060955040426

42445CB00011B/1169